UNUSUAL NIGHTS IN PARIS

Jean-Laurent Cassely

Jonglez Publishing

The guide *Unusual Nights in Paris* is the result of the observation that, between the traditional dinner with friends, trips to the theatre, cinema or opera, and nights spent in trendy bars or clubs, evenings out in the city were all beginning to seem the same …

To break this monotony, we have sampled Parisian nightlife over a few years and selected the most amazing, unusual and unexpected venues, ambiences or activities.

This guide is the fruit of our lengthy nocturnal wanderings around the capital: we took immense pleasure in its conception and hope that you will enjoy exploring these places as much as we did.

Between the start of our research and the publication of this book, several places have no doubt closed. Others, inevitably, will disappear in their turn … So go and visit them soon!

Comments about this guide and its contents, as well as information about places we have failed to include here, are welcome. They will allow us to enrich future editions of the guide.

Don't hesitate to write to us:
• Éditions Jonglez, 17, boulevard du Roi, 78000 Versailles, France
• E-mail: infos@jonglezpublishing.com

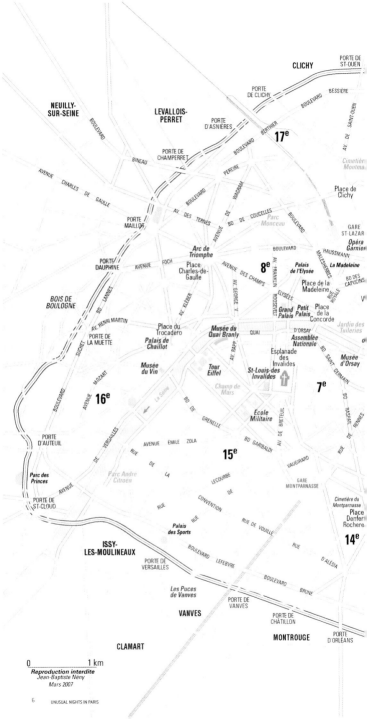

NEUILLY-SUR-SEINE

LEVALLOIS-PERRET

CLICHY

PORTE DE ST-OUEN

PORTE DE CLICHY

BOULEVARD BESSIÈRE

AV. DE SAINT-OUEN

PORTE D'ASNIÈRES

BOULEVARD BERTHIER

17^e

Cimetière Montmartre

PORTE DE CHAMPERRET

BINEAU

BOULEVARD PEREIRE

AVENUE CHARLES DE GAULLE

BOULEVARD WAGRAM

Place de Clichy

AV. DES TERNES

AVENUE DE WAGRAM

BD. DE COUCELLES

Parc Monceau

BOULEVARD

GARE ST-LAZAR

PORTE MAILLOT

Arc de Triomphe

BOULEVARD HAUSSMANN

Opéra Garnier

La Madeleine

PORTE DAUPHINE

AVENUE FOCH

Place Charles-de-Gaulle

AVENUE DES CHAMPS

8^e

AV. FRANKLIN

Palais de l'Elysée

Place de la Madeleine

BD DES CAPUCINS

RUE ROYALE

V

BOIS DE BOULOGNE

BD. LANNES

AV. KLÉBER

ÉLYSÉES

ROOSEVELT

Grand Palais

Petit Palais

Place de la Concorde

Jardin des Tuileries

AV. HENRI MARTIN

AVENUE DES CHAMPS

AV. GEORGE V.

Place du Trocadéro

Musée du Quai Branly

QUAI

D'ORSAY

PORTE DE LA MUETTE

Palais de Chaillot

AV. RAPP

Assemblée Nationale

Musée d'Orsay

SUCHET

Musée du Vin

Tour Eiffel

St-Louis-des Invalides

Esplanade des Invalides

BD SAINT GERMAIN

7^e

BOULEVARD MOZART

AVENUE

Champ de Mars

La Seine

BD. DE GRENELLE

École Militaire

AV. DE BRETEUIL

BD. RASPAIL

RUE DE RENNES

16^e

DE VERSAILLES

RUE

AVENUE EMILE ZOLA

DE

LA

BD GARIBALDI

VAUGIRARD

PORTE D'AUTEUIL

Parc André Citroën

15^e

LECOURBE

DE

GARE MONTPARNASSE

Cimetière du Montparnasse

Parc des Princes

AVENUE

RUE

CONVENTION

RUE DE VOUILLE

Place Denfert Rochere

PORTE DE ST-CLOUD

Palais des Sports

RUE

14^e

BOULEVARD LEFEBVRE

RUE

D'ALÉSIA

PORTE DE VERSAILLES

Les Puces de Vanves

BOULEVARD BRUNE

ISSY-LES-MOULINEAUX

PORTE DE VANVES

VANVES

PORTE DE CHATILLON

MONTROUGE

PORTE D'ORLEANS

CLAMART

0 _____ 1 km

Reproduction interdite
Jean-Baptiste Nény
Mars 2007

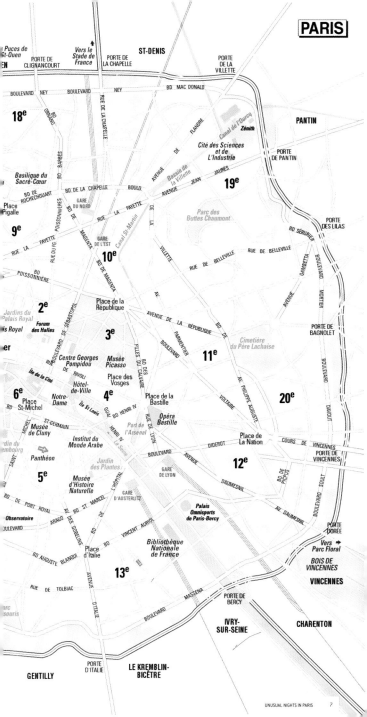

CONTENTS

CONTENTS

INDEXES

CERCLE SUÉDOIS

242, rue de Rivoli 75001 Paris
- Métro: Concorde
- Tel: 01 42 60 76 67
- www.cercle-suedois.com
- Open to the public on the second and last Wednesdays of the month, 18.00–21.00

Swedish chic

Marvellous! Twice each month, only two steps from Place de la Concorde, the extremely chic Cercle Suédois, founded in 1891, welcomes readers of this guide for an exclusive evening.

From the street, a discreet plaque indicates the existence of a Swedish and Norwegian club. Go up to the second floor and open the door on the right. At reception, the high-spirited Gunilla Poulet collects your contribution of €8 that lets you in for an amazing evening. Down the hall to the right, a grand salon in the classical style features a friendly though very professional jazz band. Louise Agerman, the dynamic and friendly manager of this select club, even sings on occasion, in English.

Behind the musicians, a door opens into a historic room: it was here, on 27 November 1895 and upon a desk that still remains in its original spot, that Alfred Nobel, the inventor of dynamite, drafted his equally explosive will setting up the famous Nobel Prize. Lastly, just next door, is the bar which is a favourite meeting-place for Swedish expatriates and French Swedophiles. The selection of vodkas and beers explains the often jovial state of the highly distinguished members in their impeccable suits and ties.

The general atmosphere, out of another era, is a delight for visiting aesthetes and those who enjoy off-beat surroundings. The walls are adorned with numerous canvases by Swedish artists, including Zorn, Grünewald, Dardel, and more recently Lennart Jirlow.

APÉRO COQUIN

11, rue du Marché Saint-Honoré 75001 Paris
• Métro: Pyramides or Tuileries
• Tel: 01 40 41 04 06
• Thursday evening 18.00–21.00
• Booking required
• E-mail: contact@yobaparis.com
• www.yobaparis.com

A frontrunner in the current fad for "sex toys", a neologism regrouping dildos and vibrators, the Yoba boutique explicitly targets young and trendy Parisians.

Choose a sex toy over a glass of champagne

Reserved exclusively for women, these "naughty evenings" accompanied by aperitifs ensure a discretion often lacking in the numerous sex shops crowding the Pigalle neighbourhood …

An ordinary building on a quiet street … No. 11 rue du Marché Saint-Honoré reveals none of its secrets to the unsuspecting passer-by. Yet, once you pass through the carriage entrance, at the rear of the courtyard you'll find a rather elegant-looking little boutique. On Thursday evenings from 18.00, a glass of champagne in their hand and a marshmallow in their mouth, women can take their time rummaging through all the different sex toys on display, without fear of being leered at by some pervert. Yoba has also spared a thought for those who want to use their charms without having recourse to sex toys and designed its own line of lingerie, also on sale.

In the room behind the shop, the atmosphere is even more muted, and more intimate. There you can browse or buy books explaining the right way to caress your man according to a gay expert, or offering updated versions of the Kama Sutra. Eavesdropping on conversations between the saleswomen and customers can be entertaining: "Let me assure you that in this position, an orgasm is guaranteed!" At Yoba, you can talk about anything without taboos, savour the different colours, or compare and even feel the different shapes available, because as the old saying goes, "it's not size that counts".

A TRASHY TUPPERWARE PARTY?

In the tradition of the famous Tupperware parties, Yoba also offers to organize its "*apéros coquins*" in your own home.

LOUVRE TOUR FROM A "SPECIAL VIEWPOINT"

- Métro: Palais Royal-Musée du Louvre
- Group visits, advance booking only • Information and reservations: Bruno de Baecque
- Tel: 06 82 29 37 44 or 01 42 01 37 16
- E-mail: bruno.debaecque@wanadoo.fr
- http://perso.orange.fr/vusoucetangle
- Admission: from 150 for a group of 10 (sliding scale for larger numbers)

The most beautiful bottoms in Paris

The most beautiful bottoms in Paris are to be found neither at the Baron nor in the shopping streets of Saint-Germain-des-Prés, but in the Louvre museum: the prestigious institution has gathered a truly impressive number of buttocks, breasts and male members.

Visibly inspired by the subject, a few years ago Bruno de Baecque put together a highly enjoyable tour based around the theme of "the most beautiful bottoms in the Louvre".

Supplied upon arrival with a Venetian mask attached to a wooden stick, each participant can shamelessly stare to their heart's content at the choicest bits. This also spares those who may come across acquaintances lingering late at the Louvre (see page 133) from the risk of being identified as an oddball …

Bruno de Baecque being an authentic national guide, stops at selected works are aimed not simply to satisfy erotic desires, but also allow him to dwell on more classical details of art history: the techniques of Michelangelo and Delacroix, or the secrets of Ingres and his Grande Odalisque with her four extra vertebrae.

After an inevitable detour to see the Venus of Milo, the superb but disturbing statue of *Hermaphroditos* Asleep is probably one of the high points of the evening: if you have noticed, on one side, the barely disguised genitals of a beautiful young man, you can't help feeling surprised, circling the statue, at seeing the sublime buttocks perfectly carved in marble, and above all, the very pretty and marvellously proportioned breasts …

STATUE OF *HERMAPHRODITOS ASLEEP*

A Roman work of art from the Imperial era (2nd century AD), the statue of Hermaphroditos Asleep rests on a magnificent marble mattress sculpted in 1608 by Bernini. For a long time it belonged to the Borghese collection, until Napoleon I bought most of the pieces from his brother-in law, Camillo Borghese, who had fallen heavily into debt. The statue came to the Louvre at the beginning of the 19th century, along with over three hundred marbles from the same collection.

HERMAPHRODITUS

Son of Hermes and Aphrodite, the young Hermaphroditus rejected the advances of the nymph of the fountain of Salmacis. She, unforgiving, could not accept this refusal and persuaded Zeus to let her body be forever united with that of Hermaphroditus.

ALLAN KARDEC

FONDATEVR
DE LA
PHILOSOPHIE SPIRITE

———

TOVT EFFET A VNE CAVSE
TOVT EFFET INTELLIGENT
A VNE CAVSE
INTELLIGENTE
LA PVISSANCE DE LA
CAVSE EST EN RAISON
DE LA GRANDEVR
DE L'EFFET

CLAIRVOYANT EXPERIENCE AT USFIPES
(UNION SCIENTIFIQUE FRANCOPHONE POUR L'INVESTIGATION PSYCHIQUE ET L'ÉTUDE DE LA SURVIVANCE)

Salle Psyché / André Dumas, shared entrance with garage, end of corridor
15, rue Jean-Jacques Rousseau 75001 Paris
• Métro: Palais Royal, Musée du Louvre or Etienne Marcel; RER: Les Halles
• Tel: 01 42 33 37 44 • E-mail: info@usfipes.org • www.usfipes.org
• Open Friday at 18.30 • Admission: €8, members €6

Martine has two unscrupulous brothers who are doing their best to steal her share of the inheritance, George has a non-existent love life, while Sylvie has been se-

*Live from
the other side*

cretly in love with her colleague at work for two years now … They were total strangers to you, but, once on USFIPES premises, various aspects of their life will be revealed to an audience of about fifty people. All this is completely normal; you are simply taking part in a collective clairvoyance session.

Here's how it works: each participant lays an object in front of the lectern at the start of the consultation. The medium will make use of these items to tell each volunteer (spending about ten minutes on each person) about their past, their present, and sometimes their future. For the hour and a half session, each of them will thus receive a psychic check-up, in the esteemed presence of Allan Kardec, the founding father of spiritualism in France, whose bust is placed behind the medium.

As most people are seeking advice on what to do, the speaker, endowed with a highly developed sense of observation and great verbal fluency, not to say glibness, undergoes successive transformations, becoming an estate agent ("Madame, you mustn't be too greedy, you've inflated the price of your farm in Brittany"), an employment counsellor ("You're starting a business, better make sure all the paperwork is filed beforehand"), a doctor ("Have regular checkups"), and girlfriend ("With a shy man, madame, you must take the initiative").

The audience is mostly female and over 50, the atmosphere is relaxed and cheerful, and the medium doesn't hesitate to pile on the details when she senses that listeners are hungry to know more about the personal life of a "consultee". There is plenty of laughter and any initial nervousness about finding yourself in the middle of a cult meeting soon fades as you become engaged by the participants who have come to seek a clearer view of their tormented lives.

Note that these collective consultations are just one of the many conference themes organized by the association. The Coué method, yoga, Chinese astrology, karma and the subconscious also feature on the programme.

The Société Française d'Études des Phénomènes Psychiques [SFEPP – French Society for the Study of Psychic Phenomena] organizes similar medium sessions, Wednesday at 18.30.

22, rue Paulin Méry 75013 Paris • Métro: Place d'Italie
• Tel (voice mail): 01 45 88 30 25 • E-mail: g.delanne@hotmail.fr
• http://gabriel.delanne.over-blog.com • Admission: €8

MAACHI DJELANI

40, rue Coquillière 75001 Paris
- Métro: Les Halles
- Tel/Fax: 01 42 33 57 47
- Open daily 10.00–20.00. All night, when the moon is full
- www.lookmaachine.com

Hairdresser
of the full moon

On nights when the moon is full, curious night birds who've managed to avoid the effects of alcohol or other illicit substances may be surprised to see people getting their hair cut at 4 or 5 in the morning.

In his ultra-cool hairdressing salon near Les Halles, Djélani Maachi is actually practising an old belief that hair grows back faster when the moon is full (and more slowly the next day). "Hair can grow as much as 2.5 cm instead of the usual one centimetre per month," he says. It's tempting to believe him, and if you need further convincing just go along to the salon when the moon is full.

While the street sleeps, Monsieur Maachi, scissors and comb in hand, cuts steadily through the early hours. His clientele come from all over: "Sometimes I don't close all night," claims the hairdresser.

Recently, our friend Maachi, who also does hair for celebrities, took a gamble on another idea to make his business viable during the day – the "relookage" [make-over]. "I was the first hairdresser to use information technology." His salon in fact looks more like a film studio with its computers and plasma screen. Starting from a simple photo and applying powerful software, he gives you a whole new look based on the resulting picture.

FULL MOON LEGENDS

Popular beliefs associate a number of occurrences with the night of the full moon. Apart from making your hair grow faster, encouraging criminals to act on their impulses (while people with mental illness find their symptoms get worse), and giving those with suicidal tendencies the courage to do away with themselves, other legends abound.

For example, more births are supposed to take place (scientific studies in fact show this to be statistically false), and certain gardening jobs (cuttings, grafts, etc.) are said to benefit, which is quite possible because the full moon gives off a considerable amount of luminous energy. Some people even plant seeds only when the moon is waxing and tubers only when it is waning ...

Surfaces exposed to moonlight are also thought to grow shinier. At least that's the claim put forward by Berluti, the luxury footwear manufacturer: made-to-measure shoes are laid out in the rays of the waxing moon to acquire their legendary patina.

LA CAVE À POÈMES

Salle Bohème, Théâtre des Déchargeurs
3, rue des Déchargeurs 75001 Paris
• Métro: Châtelet
• Information: Gérard Trougnou • Tel: 01 74 61 04 41
• Open Monday 20.00–23.00 • Fee (admission, snack, drinks): €8
• E-mail: galtroug@msn.com • http://cave-a-poemes.org

Versifying vault

Although it has held sessions for the past thirteen years in the basement of the Théâtre des Déchargeurs, "La Cave à Poèmes" [Poem Cellar] is not listed anywhere on the theatre's programme. Comfortably installed in this cool underground chamber, a former vault built in the 12th century, the Monday night poets, anxious to preserve the high standard of their verbal exchanges made possible by their limited number (about twenty), are recruited solely by word of mouth.

According to a pre-set agenda accessible on the club's website, each Monday is devoted to a different theme (journeys, childhood, idleness, eroticism, etc.), or to a poet, dead or living. The second part of the evenings is freestyle, where each participant can recite whatever they please.

The average age is rather high. "You know, it's not really an evening for young things down here!" one regular member warned straight away, as if anticipating inevitable disappointment on the part of any under-30 visitor. Yet, La Cave à Poèmes does give youth pride of place: Arthur Rimbaud, who died at the age of 37, and Jules Laforgue, who died at 27, are admirably read aloud by the participants, who may become lyrical, sombre or possessed, but are always full of conviction – and convincing. It's a far cry from tiresome classroom lessons on rhyming and the structure of the sonnet. No one here provides explanations of the text, only the interpretation and the beauty of the verse matters.

Some prefer to recite their own creations before this particularly attentive audience. Newcomers are not obliged to express themselves, but there is a participatory atmosphere and people will encourage you to join in. During the break, you'll meet all the true fans of poetry who haunt the regular gatherings in Paris, and you'll leave with the assurance that poets' circles have not vanished from the city of letters.

The Cercle des Poètes, in the 7th *arrondissement*, also organizes poetry dinners (see page 48).

LE RELAIS DES BILLETS DOUX

Throughout its history, the Théâtre des Déchargeurs has been a favourite haunt for poetic encounters. The alchemist Nicolas Flamel is said to have stored his writings there in the 14th century. Later, the building housed a public scribe who wrote love letters for his clients and guaranteed their safe delivery in less than four hours, anywhere within the Paris city walls. That explains why the first post house in the city, installed here in the 16th century, was aptly nicknamed the Relais des "billets doux" (love letters) ... And finally, it was a poet, Vicky Messica, who founded the Théâtre des Déchargeurs in 1982.

SCREENINGS FOR SWINGERS
AT CINÉMA LE BEVERLEY

14, rue de la Ville Neuve 75002 Paris
- Métro: Bonne Nouvelle
- Tel.: 01 42 36 10 57
- Screenings reserved for couples Thursday and Saturday at 23.00
- Admission: €33 per couple on Thursday, €43 per couple on Saturday

For those who no longer enjoy swingers' clubs, there is a much more unusual and less glitzy alternative: twice each week, Cinema le Beverley organizes tremendous evenings for swingers.

Swap your partner at the movies

The Beverley, a last representative of the pornographic cinemas that moved onto the grands boulevards in the 1970s, screens vintage porno films daily in a setting that has become rare in Paris.

On Thursday and Saturday evenings, the atmosphere changes slightly, with the lonely-looking single men and seekers of sleaze being replaced by couples.

If you arrive after 23.00, don't be discouraged if you find the curtain at the main entrance already drawn shut, you can still get in at the narrow door on the side.

Welcomed at the ticket counter by a man so polite that you begin to doubt what kind of evening lies in store, you then discover the cinema itself, showing a somewhat worn-out film to an audience that has also seen better days …

Gathered at the rear of the hall, the couples quickly seem to lose interest in events on the screen, and anyway the soundtrack has been cut to let the audience express itself freely …

On your first visit, it might be best to remain quietly apart; if curious you can always have a look on the way to the toilets, which you have to pass in front of the entire crowd to reach. If you're tempted you can then join in the fun.

For purists, let us make clear that the practice here is officially known as "*côte-à-côtisme*" (side-by-sideism), rather than "*mélangisme*" (mixing) or "*échangisme*" (swapping). We leave you to judge the subtle nuances of these different terms.

CONFÉRENCE BERRYER

Palais de Justice
2, boulevard du Palais 75002 Paris
• Métro: Cité or Saint-Michel
• About once a month, starting at 21.00. Turn up in front of the Palais from
19.30, with your invitation • Information and invitations: http://www.
laconference.net/laconference.html

Celebrity debates at the Palais de Justice

The Berryer conferences are both enjoyable and unforgettable events that take place in the normally anxiety-ridden atmosphere of the Palais de Justice, transformed on these occasions into a bizarre spectacle comparable to one of French satirist Pierre Desproges' famous harangues. Once a month, young Parisian lawyers gather to hear an oratorical contest to which celebrities from the arts, politics and media are invited. Held in the Salle des Criées of the Palais, the "Berryer" traditionally commences with a "report", often a mordant portrait of the evening's guest of honour, written by one of the twelve conference organizers. Then, returning to the evening's theme, two candidates are supposed to speak as brilliantly as possible on slightly crazy subjects. The surreal situations that result are often hilarious. Here are some examples: writer Anna Gavalda, invited to listen to the candidates expound on the subject, "Should we want someone to be waiting for us somewhere?" (an allusion to the title of one of Gavalda's bestselling works); singer Florent Pagny, who attended a debate on the theme, "Can Pagny pay for anything more than the freedom of thought?" (Pagny was under investigation for tax evasion), while politician François Baroin had to put up with a session on "Will Harry Potter save Chiracdom?" (one of the youngest members of President Chirac's government, Baroin wears round spectacles) … Jean-Marie Messier, Nicolas Sarkozy, Laurent Fabius, Philippe Sollers and Bernard-Henri Lévy have also been willing victims in recent years.

If the candidate speakers, some of them recruited from outside the legal profession, rarely achieve the degree of eloquence demonstrated by the lawyers organizing the conference, the critique of their debating skills by said lawyers is, on the other hand, a brilliant lesson in wit and obtuseness. The twelve pros, used to defending all sorts of clients during their working week, have the time of their lives taking it all out on the poor candidate. Unconvincing performances are singled out, but the accusers go much further and the miserable wretch in question can be attacked for his or her physique, dress sense, or name … Anything goes, and the sadistic audience is often delighted by this stylistic exercise, carried out with subtle but often painful humour. Not to be missed.

BERRYER, AN OUTSTANDING LAWYER

Pierre-Antoine Berryer (1790–1868), member of the Académie Française, politician, lawyer and president of the French Bar, is still renowned for his independent mind, his liking for a good challenge, and the quality of his pleas in court. He was the defender of Marshal Ney, Generals Debelle and Cambronne, Louis-Napoléon Bonaparte, Chateaubriand and numerous organs of the French press.

BIBLIOTHÈQUE DES AMIS DE L'INSTRUCTION
OF THE 3ᴿᴰ ARRONDISSEMENT

54, rue de Turenne 75003 Paris
• Métro: Chemin Vert or Saint-Paul
• Open Saturday 15.00–19.00, first and third Sundays of the month 10.00–13.00, and by appointment
• Evening readings certain Thursdays at 19.30, admission free as long as places are available
• Tel: 01 42 71 03 43
• www.bai.asso.fr

Evening readings from another century

The Marais neighbourhood, 1861. Local workers and craftsmen gathered together books of their own choosing and founded the Bibliothèque des Amis de l'Instruction [Library of the Friends of Learning]. Its principal novelty was that the books could be borrowed to read at home, thereby giving the labouring classes their first opportunity to study works in their spare time. The library's deliciously quaint name illustrates perfectly the utopia of "popular learning" that motivated its founders. An additional period detail: membership for women, who could also consult the books, was half-price …

To give this veritable academy of popular literacy a more active role and a higher profile, the library association has organized evening readings or lectures for the past twenty years. Six to eight lectures are thus scheduled certain Thursdays at 19.30. These offer an opportunity to enter this timeless institution, which is somewhat severe-looking but also marvellously strange.

The library has remained fairly private; only the association members and a few local residents seem to be aware of its existence, but this does not prevent the evening readings from being well-attended. You can thus find elderly people sitting on the floor in a corner, if all the chairs are taken, eager to hear the proceedings … The lectures, offered by experts, usually teachers or writers, focus on literary and social issues of the 19th century. "Reading in the time of Balzac and Eugène Sue", "Women writers and naturalism", "The century of the Saint-Simonians", or "Women travellers in the 19th century", were all part of the programme in 2007.

Most of the 20,000 volumes in the original collection are still kept here, but lending has been stopped in order preserve the copies. But the novels, essays and magazines from the early period can be consulted at the library on Saturday afternoons, as well as every other Sunday.

RAIDD BAR

23, rue du Temple 75003 Paris
- Métro: Rambuteau
- www.raiddbar.com
- Open daily 17.00–2.00

If those of you seeking the unusual only have time to visit one gay bar in the Marais neighbourhood, try the Raidd.

There was a guy taking a shower ...!

Unlike others, the Raidd Bar is not merely a meeting-place or a pickup joint for homosexuals.

Every evening at 20.30, 21.30, 22.30 and 23.30, a handsome and perfectly proportioned young man actually takes his shower before the watchful eyes of the excited crowd.

Protected by a wall of glass from any potential urge to touch, it's all there before your very eyes: the showerhead, the running water, the bar of soap that our man takes a sly pleasure in running sensually over his entire body. Only his genitals remain invisible, as modesty but above all the law requires.

Except for the virile member that is only hinted at, being draped in a towel that just barely remains decent, you get to see everything. The buttocks press conspicuously against the glass and the hand lingers deliberately at the most lubricious spots, offering the perfect show for the Marais scene. The bar is packed every evening.

For those who haven't had enough, it's time to go down to the toilet in the basement. Place yourself calmly in front of one of the urinals. Look straight ahead. A video screen is facing you. Take a closer look and you'll see a partial view of yourself. This is the right moment for some young Adonis to decide to use another urinal. Stand still, looking straight ahead. Surprise! The video screen gives you the refreshing impression that the young Adonis in question is watching you intently ... But rest assured, he'll be getting the same impression on his side ...

Accessible to curious women, too, but only if (properly) accompanied.

CARGO CLUB APÉRO AT LIBRAIRIE ULYSSE

26, rue Saint-Louis en l'Ile 75004 Paris
- Métro: Pont Marie or Sully-Morland
- First Wednesday of the month from 18.30
- Bring a bottle, plastic cups, and something to nibble
- Information: Tel: 01 43 25 17 35
- www.ulysse.fr

Once a month the Ulysse bookshop, specializing in travel literature, organizes evening aperitifs for fans of freighter voyages.

Prepare for a freighter trip

For those who have only travelled by train or plane, you should know that most freighters, or even modern-day container ships, usually have cabins available for travellers with a spirit of adventure. The advantage is that it allows more time to experience the journey, at least according to one organizer of freighter trips. The drawback is that it's much more expensive than travel by air, for a journey ten times longer!

Since not many ordinary travel agencies bother with this niche market, the Cargo Club *apéro* is the ideal place to prepare for the next trip. Young students or retired people, dreaming of escape to faraway shores, these candidates for a freighter voyage are keen on exotic destinations: Alexandria, Singapore, the Panama Canal, Fort-de-France …

Using the same routes as the merchant navy, the itineraries proposed do indeed sound adventurous and inevitably summon up the quaint charms of those pages in a Tintin album where one sees the intrepid reporter departing for Port Said, Shanghai or the Americas …

For those really tempted, passengers are usually housed in officers' quarters, take their meals with the crew, and sometimes enjoy use of the ship's leisure facilities (gym, ping-pong table, library, etc.).

But beware: despite the massive size of certain container ships or oil tankers, sea sickness often afflicts those unused to a moving deck …

The concept of the Cargo Club *apéro* regularly attracts some colourful characters who help to make these events quite lively …

But please don't go thumbing through the books on the shelves. The bookseller, fed up with finding red wine stains on her stock, only allows short trips inside for fresh supplies.

ULYSSE, THE "CLUB" BOOKSHOP

Catherine Domain founded this bookshop in 1971. But as the homepage of the shop's website informs you, she is also a member of the Société des Explorateurs and the Club International des Grands Voyageurs, as well as the founder of the Cargo Club and the Club Ulysse des Petites Iles du Monde. To become a member of this last and very exclusive group, you must be the owner or resident of an island, and one small enough to walk all the way around in less than 24 hours!

GROUP DIDGERIDOO CLASSES
WITH THE VENT DU RÊVE ASSOCIATION

9, rue Quincampoix 75004 Paris
- Métro: Châtelet-Les Halles
- Monday 19.30–21.30 at Imprévu Café
- Annual membership fee: €30
- E-mail: infos@ventdureve.net
- http://ventdureve.blogspot.com

Commune to the sound of didgeridoos

I f one Monday evening you venture into the basement of the Imprévu Café, you may believe you've stumbled on the secret meeting-place of a cult summoning up dark forces with their otherworldly vibrations … But in fact it's just a music class organized by an association: for the last decade, fans of the didgeridoo have gathered at this café in the Marais to practise playing their favourite instrument and improve their breathing technique.

Mastering the didgeridoo, which is above all a rhythmic instrument, requires a certain degree of breathing discipline to achieve a powerful and continuous sound, although you don't need to learn scales or immerse yourself in the theory of harmony.

A little goodwill should therefore be enough to let you to commune musically with the members of the association, especially since beginners are welcome and receive individual tutoring until they are good enough to join in with the collective vibes.

Newcomers are asked to pay the annual membership fee, but the amount is reasonable and you can start with an instrument made from PVC piping, before contemplating buying a more traditional version or – why not? – making an initiatory journey to meet the aborigines of Northern Australia who use the didgeridoo in their rituals.

THE DIGERIDOO, AN INSTRUMENT UNLIKE ANY OTHER

Australian in origin, the didgeridoo in fact has some fifty names, its current one being an onomatopoeic word invented by Western colonists – "didgeridoo" seeming close to the sound they heard. Traditionally, the didgeridoo is made from a eucalyptus branch hollowed out naturally by termites, and is played exclusively by men to accompany the singing at various Aboriginal ceremonies (funerals, storytelling, entertainments, etc.).

For several years now, New Age adepts have also made use of the powerful vibrations emitted by the didgeridoo to perform sonic massages up and down the spine …

DANS LE NOIR

51, rue Quincampoix 75004 Paris
- RER: Châtelet-Les Halles
- Tel: 01 42 77 98 04 • www.danslenoir.com
- Open Monday to Saturday. 3 services daily: 12.30, 20.00, 22.00; Sunday brunch, 12.00–17.00
- Dans le Noir bar: open daily 17.30–19.30, then midnight–2.00
- Surprise menu: €21 to €35

Dine in pitch blackness

"We provide a playful, sensorial, and human adventure, perhaps a little crazy, but that's exactly why it should work. It has already existed in Zurich and Berlin for several years now," says Edouard de Broglie, instigator of the project. In Paris, the experience has also been tried before, but only on a temporary basis.

The idea is that of dining in complete darkness, guided throughout by blind people who take on the role of waiters for the occasion. It's an exceptional way of living an extraordinary experience, but also and above all, for a short while, of putting yourself in the shoes of a blind person and hence better understanding, very concretely, the real nature of the disability.

Some evenings, a discussion may strike up with your host or hostess, giving them a chance to raise the awareness of the wider public, but also giving them more contact with sighted people, not always as frequent as it might seem …

The evening begins at the cloakroom, where you are supposed to leave any object capable of emitting even a little light: lighters, watches, mobile phones … so the darkness really will be total. The same rule applies to the organizers who, one evening, served sushi that turned out to be fluorescent in the dark!

Shortly after, a blind waiter or waitress arrives to take guests by the hand and guide them to their seats. That's when things start in earnest. When you have to pour wine in your glass, or try to stab food with your fork …

Whether your eyes are open or shut, it makes no difference. It's pitch black! Soon, conversations get going as questions begin to flow: "Is there apple in this …?", "That wouldn't be a fig tart, would it?" It's only on the way out, when you get a chance to read the actual composition of the surprise menu, that you come to realize the degree to which we are all conditioned by the sight of food.

During dinner, you find yourself touching the shoulder or arm of another customer … although you were just fumbling for your glass or your plate. Tuesday evenings are even reserved for singles; the place is clearly a winner for fans of "blind dates"!

Only one negative note: the dining room is very noisy, because people talk much louder when they can't see! Lastly, some will say that the cooking lacks flavour, which is a matter of taste, but really the food is quite decent and in any case not the main reason for coming here.

« CINOCHE VIDÉO » HOME SCREENINGS
OF FILMS AND DOCUMENTARIES BY MARIA KOLEVA

43, boulevard Saint-Michel 75005 Paris
• Métro: Saint-Michel; RER: Luxembourg
• Tel: 01 47 00 61 31 • Admission free
• Weekly programmes published in the Officiel des Spectacles ("séances spéciales"), Pariscope ("séances exceptionnelles") and posted at 43 boulevard Saint-Michel • Cassettes and books by the director are also on sale at Harmattan bookshop, 21 bis rue des Écoles

*Living room
agit-prop*

F or those who are sick and tired of going to impersonal cinema complexes to see bland, glossy films, Maria Koleva, a Bulgarian living in Paris since the 1970s, has come up with an intriguing idea for weekly screenings of her highly politicized work.

To find out what's on, buy a copy of *Pariscope* or *Officiel des Spectacles* for the times of screenings. At the appointed hour, show up at 43 boulevard Saint-Michel. Ring Koleva's bell, go up to the third floor, ring again at the door on the left, and be sure to wipe your feet on the mat – an interest in underground cinema is no excuse for being a slob …

Maria Koleva enthusiastically welcomes you into her (small) living room, also used for the screenings. The huge iron object, which looks like something out of an agricultural museum, is actually a rostrum camera, an antique piece of apparatus abandoned by the French TF1 television network and now used by Koleva in her film editing.

Driven by an apparently insatiable need to document anything happening in far left political circles (from demos against the reform of unemployment benefits to general assemblies for a more equitable, sustainable economy), Maria Koleva has made some five hundred films, and always has yet another project under way. Within this copious body of work, you'll find political documentaries, militant fictional parodies, and theatre classes by Antoine Vitez, filmed in 1976 at the Conservatoire National d'Art Dramatique in Paris.

On the evening we visited, she was showing two satirical short fictions from her series, *Grandeur et misère de la société de consommation*. These consisted of 20 minute takes, with a single actress playing all the roles, a minimalist set and a surreal script. The main targets of her sardonic parodies tend to be Parisian film producers and journalists, corrupt and brainwashed members of the bourgeoisie serving the interests of American capitalism – much to the delight of an audience already sharing Koleva's political convictions!

Complaining about the lack of recognition her work has received from official bodies and about being relegated to the underground network, the filmmaker –extremely talkative as well as being an activist – likes to exaggerate the conspiracy aimed at silencing her … You can learn more about her eclectic theories on politics, life and the dramatic arts in film and theatre by reading the innumerable presentations on her works that she distributes before, during and after the show.

Unique.

THE BED AT SHAKESPEARE & COMPANY
THE ENGLISH-LANGUAGE BOOKSHOP

37, rue de la Bûcherie 75005 Paris
• Métro or RER: Saint-Michel
• Readings of texts and meetings with authors Monday at 19.00 (in English)
• Tel: 01 43 25 40 93
• Bookshop open daily, from noon to midnight
• www.shakespeareco.org

*Take a nap
in a bookshop*

Although everyone in Paris has heard about Shakespeare & Company bookshop, few know that there are beds available on the first floor for readers or anyone wanting to take a nap in more peaceful surroundings than those offered by a Parisian bench.

As all the employees working there like to repeat, "Shakespeare & Company has grown from a bookstore into an institution". This remains so today, to the extent that this shop selling books in English is perhaps, paradoxically, more representative of the mythical Latin Quarter than its French-language neighbours offering Descartes or Voltaire …

The books, arranged in a seemingly random manner, spill from the shelves onto the shop floor. Visitors are welcome to read them on the premises for as long as they like, notably sitting on one of the benches out front.

On the ground level, a hollow dug into the floor, the remnant of a well, is regularly filled with coins by superstitious customers making a wish. The walls are covered with souvenir photos, postcards addressed to the proprietor, little notes of appreciation, and philosophical musings … It's a joyful Anglo-Saxon muddle of a shop, a private home, and a neighbourhood social centre.

The bookshop was founded in 1951 by George Whitman, a literary traveller of the Beat generation who compares his own personality to that of Don

Quixote and his life to that of Dostoyevsky's Idiot ...

Among those who have posted their impressions on the walls, one called the shop a "bohemian utopia", while another said it was "a socialist laboratory disguised as a bookstore", no doubt alluding to the legendary hospitality of the master of the house, who has allowed dozens of young writers passing through Paris to stay as guests on the first floor, long enough to finish their literary projects.

The reputation of George Whitman – whose daughter, Sylvia, now runs the shop – is such that no English-language guide to Paris omits reference to him. Shakespeare & Company was even listed by an Australian newspaper as one of the five best bookshops in the world!

LATE-NIGHT BOOKSHOPS

La Hune :
170, bd Saint-Germain 75006 Paris. Métro: Saint-Germain-des-Prés
• Open Monday to Saturday until 23.45 • Tel: 01 45 48 35 85

La Passerelle :
3, rue Saint-Hubert 75011 Paris. Métro Saint-Maur
• Open Tuesday to Friday until 1.00, Saturday until 2.00
• Tel: 01 43 57 04 82
• www.alapasserelle.org

Librairie Tschann :
125, boulevard du Montparnasse 75006 Paris
• Métro: Vavin
• Open Tuesday to Saturday 10.00–22.00; until 20.00 Monday
• Tel: 01 43 35 42 05
Founded in 1929 by Louis Tschann and his wife, who were prominent members of the Montparnasse artistic and intellectual scene at the time, the Tschann bookshop specializes in literary works, poetry and social sciences. Readings are organized at the shop on a regular basis.

THE ROCKY HORROR PICTURE SHOW

Cinéma Studio Galande
42, rue Galande 75005 Paris
• Métro: Maubert-Mutualité
• Evenings organized around the film on Friday (Irrational Masters) and
Saturday (The Sweet Transvestites), starting at 22.10 • Tel: 08 92 68 06 24
• E-mail: information@studiogalande.fr • http://www.studiogalande.fr

Everyone should see *The Rocky Horror Picture Show* at the Studio Galande at least once in their life.

A re-animated crowd

The evening does demand some advance preparation: clothes that don't mind stains, bags of flour, fresh eggs, rice, and a certain sense of irony (what the French call "*second degré*" humour; "*premier degré*" being no humour at all).

Obviously, if you're still a student, you'll fit right in: except for some stray Japanese tourists who sometimes join the party, most of those present are young Parisians from the Latin Quarter who drop by for their weekly decompression session. The keenest of them have seen the film at least a hundred times, some even more.

But more than the film itself, most of the spectators come for the "animations" organized by two troupes of volunteer actors. The term "animation" is in fact a little feeble to describe the collective madness that takes place twice weekly: armed with rice – to throw during the wedding scenes – and water – to simulate the rainstorm that takes the characters by surprise – the fans are whipped up to a frenzy by the team of actors who lead some YMCA-style choreography during the early part of the evening. Then comes the "briefing": each time the name Brad – the anti-hero of the film – is heard, the crowd is instructed to yell "Asshole!" When his fiancée is named, another appropriate epithet is applied … The Sweet Transvestites crew meanwhile enhances the film with interactive and scatological games to please those who like their humour crude and lewd. You can thus see inflatable dolls released, the mass rape of the audience simulated by the actors, and some other rather hard-core pranks. At the end of two hours of dancing, screaming and throwing all kinds of objects, you emerge exhausted, soaking, dirty, and generally all shook up … If you're still keen, the troupe invites you to have a drink with them afterwards at a nearby bar.

BIRTH OF A LEGEND …

For readers who are too young or rather out of touch, we should perhaps explain that *The Rocky Horror Picture Show* is a B- or even Z-series musical comedy, sending up the scenarios of Dracula and Frankenstein movies in a gay-friendly fashion. The mad scientist is a transsexual transvestite from Transylvania, and his creature, Rocky, is a sort of gay icon with carefully lubricated muscles …

The film's assertive kitsch has attracted a devoted cult following, first in the United States and then the rest of the world. The Studio Galande cinema in Paris has been perpetuating this daft tradition for over twenty years now.

SKYWATCHING AT THE OBSERVATOIRE
DE LA SOCIÉTÉ ASTRONOMIQUE DE FRANCE

Université de la Sorbonne
- Métro: Cluny; RER: Luxembourg
- Monday and Friday at 20.00, advance booking only (21.00 in summer)
- Admission: €5, free for members
- Information and reservations: Société Astronomique de France, 3, rue Beethoven, 75016 Paris
- Tel: 01 42 24 13 74 • www.saf-lastronomie.com

Although students at the Sorbonne pass beneath it every day, few of them know what really lies hidden under the cupola of the tower on rue Saint-Jacques. Within the university precinct, it houses an extraordinary observatory built at the beginning of the 20th century. Run by the Société Astronomique de France (SAF), it in fact consists of two cupolas, the higher of which is still used for observation. Reaching a height of 39 m, it offers a splendid panorama of Paris.

Ambiance worthy of Tintin and the Shooting Star

Despite urban pollution and interference from the city lights, the 153 mm telescope which takes pride of place under the cupola is quite adequate for admiring the moon and the planets of the solar system. If you manage to get in, you'll probably spend a fascinating evening there.

The problems start with the obligatory reservation at SAF headquarters: you'll need to pray for an available spot in the near future, because the two weekly visits are limited to only five people at a time … Once you've booked, you're still at the mercy of fate, and in particular, the weather: depending on conditions, and thus the chance of observing the sky, these evenings are often cancelled at the last minute. If you're trying to impress a prospective lover with an unusual night out, you'd better be ready with a back-up plan!

Once the date is confirmed, the magic begins: in a dark corner of the university, when most of the students have gone home, the chosen few gather. You then take a lift up to the observatory workshop, where keen astronomers make their telescope mirrors by hand. After having more or less understood the guide's explanations, you then have to take the stairs up two more floors to reach the cupola.

The opening system, which pivots through 360°, still operates by means of the original mechanism using chains and pulleys: your guide turns a crank whose characteristic sound will probably summon up images of *Tintin in The Shooting Star* album.

Unforgettable.

The Sorbonne observatory is the only one in the Paris region accessible to the public on a regular basis: those at Port-Royal and Meudon only open their doors on rare occasions.

INCOGNITO

16, Guénégaud 75006 Paris
- Métro: Odéon
- Tel: 01 43 25 78 38
- Open to members 24 hours
- E-mail: artclub@incognito.vu

A gallery open 24 hours, where members hold the keys ...

Here's an art gallery that really trusts its members: they're given the keys to the shop and can drop by whenever they please, day or night. And if you're thinking the place is always guarded, you'd be mistaken: there is no gallery owner, no sales personnel, or even cameras. Just the spotlights, switched on round the clock. Located on rue Guénégaud in Saint-Germain-des-Prés, the place is called Incognito. The narrow space is only the size of a small hallway but it's impossible to miss: its candy-pink façade stands out from the rest of this drab-looking street.

Open for three years, Incognito is in fact a very exclusive club for fans of contemporary art (videos, installations, photos, paintings). For an annual subscription of €500 (deductible from the purchase price of an artwork), the club's VIP members can thus appropriate use of the gallery for the space of an often fleeting visit, since there are never more than a handful of works to be seen. Today there are about sixty members in possession of the magnetic card giving them access to these premises at any hour.

The artists on display include stars such as Armleder and Villéglé, but also up-and-coming talents Soulerin or Grancher. So if you see a shadowy figure entering the place in the middle of the night, don't call the police. It's no doubt only an insomniac art collector …

© Incognito

OTHER ART GALLERIES OPEN LATE
Galerie de AAM Coiffure
Rue Bertin-Poirée 75001 Paris
- Métro: Châtelet or Pont-Neuf
- Tel: 01 40 26 36 34

Parisians who pass by rue Bertin-Poirée may be intrigued by a little recess measuring one metre by five, in which paintings are displayed behind a window. This micro-gallery, which remains lit until 22.00, in fact continues within the hairdressing salon next door. During building work, Arnaud, the salon's owner, found himself up against a brick wall preventing him from linking up to the rest of the salon, whence the idea of doing "something" with this little place. Since he was a lover of painting, he offered artists exhibition space for a month or two. Today, it's booked up a year in advance ...

La Vitrine
Galerie Frédéric Giroux
8, rue Charlot 75003 Paris
- Métro: Saint-Sébastien-Froissart
- Tel: 01 42 71 01 02
- E-mail: info@fredericgriroux.com
- www.fredericgroux.com

In a much more professional spirit oriented towards contemporary art, the Frédéric Giroux gallery has a display window that remains lit all night, on rue Charlot. This curious white "cube" is the setting for a series of proposals from Muriel Colin-Barrand (see C.O.N.S.O.L.E., page 62), presenting works of artists that have been specially conceived for this restricted space. You'll be sure to find something satisfactory if a sudden urge for contemporary art comes over you on sleepless nights.

© Amande In

A NIGHT AT THE SENATE

Visitors' entrance at 15, rue de Vaugirard 75006 Paris
• RER: Luxembourg; Métro: Odéon
• Sessions of the French Senate open to the public Tuesday, Wednesday and Friday at 10.00, 15.00 and evenings, as seating allows
• Identity card obligatory • To find out when the evening session resumes, call the Senate's answering service: 01 42 34 20 01
• http://www.senat.fr/visite/visiter.html

A**t 15 rue de Vaugirard, French senators sit in session, largely ignored by the majority of the French people. Nevertheless, it is possible and even relatively easy to attend ordinary meetings of the upper chamber of Parliament. In the evenings, the senators generally resume their deliberations two hours after a recess is declared at the end of the afternoon. You'll need to enquire on the day to find out if the assembly is continuing to sit that night.

Late-night sittings

After showing your identity card at reception, pass through the security gate and walk across the grand courtyard to the entrance opposite. Then let yourself be guided by the officers present – usually much more numerous than visitors! – up to the second floor. You'll then be briefed about proper conduct as a spectator of parliamentary debate: "It's forbidden to shout, display banners, express any sign of approval or disapproval … or fall asleep during the session!"

Having taken in the luxurious decor of the Palais du Luxembourg, you will soon notice that the Senate's day-to-day existence is far removed from the frenetic turmoil of the political scene. On the day we visited, only a dozen senators showed up for the second reading of a bill on the management of water and aquatic environments. At the foot of the Senate president's desk, the attendants were chatting among themselves, while some senators sought distraction in the French satirical newspaper, *Le Canard Enchaîné*. "This water bill is a long and winding river!" one orator dared to utter in an effort to rouse his audience. If you find yourself growing bored or disappointed at not seeing Jean-Pierre Raffarin, Michel Charasse, or another of the Senate's stars, you can slip out (quietly) at any time.

AN EVENING AT THE NATIONAL ASSEMBLY
33, quai d'Orsay 75007 Paris • Métro: Assemblée Nationale
• Daily agenda: Assembly answering service (01 40 63 77 77)
or www.assemblee-nationale.fr/agendas/odj.asp
The public nature of debates in both chambers of the French Parliament is stipulated by Article 33 of the Constitution, but in practice it is easier to attend the Senate than the National Assembly. To see the lower chamber in action, you will need to contact your member of parliament at least a week in advance in order to be invited to a public session. Only the first ten arrivals are guaranteed access to the proceedings.
Whether at the Palais du Luxembourg or the Palais-Bourbon, the best time to go along is during major governmental crises (such as a student strike or a political-financial scandal) – the atmosphere is much more dynamic and draws a bigger crowd than more routine sessions.

"TEXTES & VOIX": EVENING READINGS
AT REID HALL

4, rue de Chevreuse 75006 Paris • Métro: Vavin
- One Monday each month at 20.00
- Tickets available from 19.30 at Librairie Tschann
  125, boulevard du Montparnasse 75006 Paris
- Tel: 01 43 35 42 05
- Information and programme: http://www.textes-et-voix.asso.fr
- Nadine Eghels: E-mail: nadine.eghels@wanadoo.fr
- Admission: €10, €5 unemployed and students

Little-known readings at Reid Hall

Since 1999, lovers of literature have had the privilege, once a month, of gathering for evening readings organized by the association Textes & Voix, in the superb Reid Hall.

Based on the observation that when books are promoted, "one mostly hears comments about the work, and only rarely its own living voice", the original idea was to listen to excerpts from a contemporary work, read by an actor in the presence of the author.

Some big names from the stage such as Daniel Mesguich, Marie-Christine Barrault and Aurélien Recoing have already performed this exercise. The readings, before an audience of about a hundred, are followed by a debate with the author, all in a very professional and technically faultless environment, remarkably so for a project run by a voluntary association.

With the assistance of the Tschann bookshop, these events take place in the magical and unfamiliar setting of Reid Hall. This venue, which encompasses an entire block between boulevard du Montparnasse, rue de Chevreuse and rue Notre-Dame-des-Champs, has belonged to New York's Columbia University since 1964.

A teaching and research centre fostering Franco-American exchanges, Reid Hall hosts the readings by Textes & Voix in its majestic lecture hall. When you cross the university's garden and inner courtyard, islands of calm and greenery only two steps away from the noisy boulevard du Montparnasse, you may feel a twinge of envy of the American students and researchers who work every day in these very picturesque surroundings.

CLUB DES POÈTES

30, rue de Bourgogne 75007 Paris
- Métro: Varenne or Invalides
- Tel: 01 47 05 06 03; www.poesie.net
- Open daily, except Saturday lunch time and Sunday
- Dinner at 20.00, show at 22.00. Dinner menu €20

Friends of poetry, bonsoir!

The Club des Poètes is one of those rare and precious venues in a city where you can enjoy the sensation, for a brief instant, of stepping outside of time.

Only a short walk from the National Assembly, Jean-Pierre Rosnay and his wife Marcelle welcome poetry lovers from around the world for a drink or dinner. There are even a few foreign enthusiasts who come regularly without speaking a word of French, but nevertheless take delight in the intimate atmosphere and the sonority of the poems declaimed there.

Created in 1961 in order to "render poetry contagious and inevitable" because it is "the anti-pollutant of mental space, the counterweight and the antidote for an existence which tends to turn us into robots" according to the website, the Club des Poètes has received visits from many renowned poets such as Pablo Neruda, Octavio Paz and Ma Desheng.

The place itself is intriguing: the massive wooden door with its small wrought-iron opening, like in the Middle Ages, forcing any latecomers who show up after the poetry sessions have begun to undergo inspection, sets a certain tone.

Although you can dine here at reasonable cost (set menus for €15 or €20), the food, typically French, is not very memorable although decent enough. The poetry lovers, most of them regulars, arrive one by one. Monsieur Rosnay, junior, fusses over his youngest child with his wife, Yasmine … The ambience could not be more familial, just like being at home, or almost, as there are books scattered all about the room and even in the toilet.

Towards 22.00, Monsieur Rosnay, senior, begins the evening's recitals: classic poems, modern poems, even ones he composed himself. Then there's a brief interval, to finish dessert, before things start up again. The lights go down, then come back on for a moment, and for nearly two hours family, regulars and more occasional visitors take turns in the spotlight, publicly reciting a poem of their choice. If the diction varies according to the performer, the pleasure of listening is always there, and the atmosphere is wonderful, alternately hushed then enthusiastic.

In order to enjoy the experience to the utmost, before coming make the effort to learn a poem and then dare to recite it aloud!

Dans le cadre de la manifestation «Ingénieurs et Poètes» et sous le Haut
Patronnage du Ministère de la Culture et de la Communication
École Nationale Supérieure de l'Électronique et de ses Applications
et Jean-Pierre Rosnay présentent

Les Illuminations

Spectacle Poésie-Musique

Rimbaud

interprété

par

le Club des
Poètes

Mozart

servi par

le Quatuor

Michel
Deneuve

Maison de Quartier de Cergy Saint-Christophe
Samedi 19 octobre 1991 à 20h30

La journée débutera à 15h par la visite de l'Axe Majeur suivie, à 17h, de la remise des
poésie ENSEA/Club des Poètes et de nouvelle ENSEA/Taille Réelle au Centre Pascal
Batignolles. Et si le cœur vous en dit, nous vous accueillerons, à 19h, aux Rencontres et
sur le thème des liens fructueux entre Science et Poésie qui précéderont ce spectacle

Prix des places (nombre limité) : 50F pour le spectacle, 70F
journée (Tarif réduit pour les étudiants et les groupes)

Réservations et renseignements à l'ENSEA-Les Plumes de l'Axe : 30
Le Club des Poètes : 47 05 06 03 ou 3615 code CLP

BP

DEFI Jeunes

OPEN STAGE AT THE FIEALD

14, rue de Trévise 75009 Paris
• Métro: Cadet or Grands-Boulevards
• Sunday at 20.30 in Théâtre Trévise, from September to June
• Information: L'Art Seine 06 64 95 97 25
• www.fieald.net
• Admission: €9/€7 (subscribers)

"Although you make money in the métro, it's more rewarding on stage!"

Every Sunday evening, just a short distance from the Folies Bergères, about a hundred Parisians crowd in front of the Théâtre Trévise. Since 1991, birth year of the "oldest open stage in Paris", the theatre hosts for the price of a cinema ticket the Festival International d'Expression Artistique Libre et … Désordonnée (FIEALD – International Festival of Free and Disorderly Artistic Expression).

For over two hours, a troupe of actors backed by a rock band and L'Art Seine technicians mastermind this bizarre ceremony that welcomes all novice performers, with no prior audition or selection.

The rotation between live music, sketches, and electrifying warm-up exercises led by the FIEALD's own team give the whole evening the feeling of a variety show. "One-man acts, musicians, circus numbers, tropic flea tamers, polyglot clowns and neighbourhood stars", the FIEALD is a festival of all genres, even if the stand-up comedian is the most commonly represented here. Indeed, Jamel Debbouze, Élie and Dieudonné, Dany Boon and Jean-Luc Lemoine have all trod the boards of the Théâtre Trévise. Some stars of one-man shows, such as Gustave Parking, the patron of FIEALD since its creation, may make surprise appearances.

Those aspiring to theatrical glory should register here at 19.30 on the dot. Sessions are often oversubscribed, so performers have to wait until the following Sunday evening, their patience finally rewarded by their first turn on stage.

Sometimes a little intimidated or even petrified by stage fright, novices forget their lines and take their prompt sheets from their pockets in a vain attempt to save face. "Well, umm, I had another gag, but I can't remember how it goes …" At the end of the performance, the house actors come on to interview the comedian, musician or duo, with the recurring question, "Do you have a gig?" Those who have something lined up bring out their album or announce that they'll be appearing at a Parisian *café-théâtre*, while those who don't … may have a long wait ahead of them.

But at least for the space of these evenings, the golden rule is: everyone has their fifteen minutes of fame. As one participant put it, "Although you make money in the métro, it's more rewarding on stage!"

CERCLE CLICHY-MONTMARTRE

84, rue de Clichy 75009 Paris
- Métro: Place-de-Clichy
- Tel: 01 48 78 32 85
- Open all year round; billiard hall 11.00–6.00 in the morning; gaming circle 16.00–6.00
- No admittance to minors; identity card obligatory

O ccupying a magnificent Art Nouveau hall, the Cercle Clichy-Montmartre is a spectacular leisure establishment that has been in existence since the 18th century. At that time, the walls enclosing the Folie Bouxière extended around the entire neighbourhood. Taken over in 1947 by the father-in-law of the present director, the place has become a gaming hall.

The colour of money

Besides amateurs who come to relax, the Cercle also welcomes some true stars of billiards. This is attested by the personal lockers of regular players, all securely padlocked. French champions train here daily, and indeed the Cercle sponsors a number of professional players.

At the rear of the hall, signs representing playing cards, lit up in neon, indicate the entrance to the gaming circle. Stud poker, blackjack, 21 and multicolore (see page 114) await the night gamblers of the Pigalle neighbourhood. It's a strange scene, indeed.

The impressive hall with its majestic mirrors almost makes the venue seem like a formal club. But the Cercle Clichy-Montmartre is anything but snobbish. The notice "Correct attire required" is purely symbolic.

ESCUALITA,
TRANSSEXUAL EVENINGS AT THE FOLIES PIGALLE

11, place Pigalle 75009 Paris
• Métro: Pigalle
• Sunday from 23.30 until dawn, and first Friday of the month
("after" party until noon)
• Non-stop in summer
• www.escualita.com
• Admission: €20, €10 with a pass (available in bars at Oberkampf,
Abbesses, République, Marais and Pigalle)

**Must
be seen
to be believed**

If you still have doubts, Escualita will confirm that Pigalle still amply deserves its international reputation. Alluding to a New York clubbing scene where transsexuals mix with riffraff from the Bronx, the Escualita evenings at the Folies Pigalle are the venue for surreal meetings between hormone-charged transsexuals, suburban slum dwellers, muscular blacks and a few stray tourists obviously out of their depth. Queens for a night, the transexuals rule the roost in these evenings in their honour: distributing kisses and letting hands wander with charming abandon, these folk (whose gender is often difficult to pin down, much to the delight of those present) are happy for the chance to show off, which is the whole reason they're here! At regular intervals, a silicon-loaded creature climbs the podium to display to the excited crowd the more or less successful outcome of their latest operation.

Some night revellers are madly enthusiastic about these evenings where excess becomes the norm. More cynical observers claim that it's simply a means for the pros working the Bois de Boulogne to drum up some extra trade. We leave you to make up your own mind.

It's an ideal way to loosen up an uptight colleague: about a third of those present are transexual, a recipe which always makes these evenings a success …

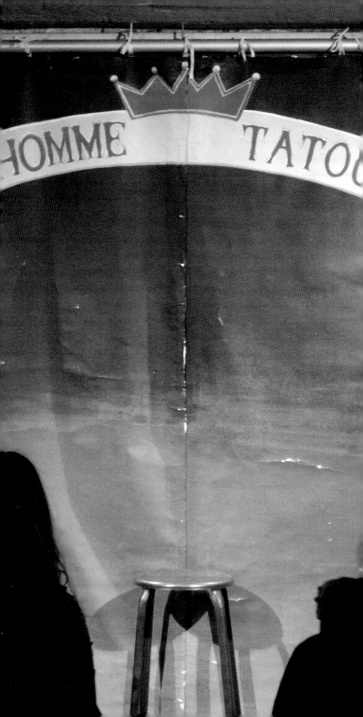

L'HOMME TATOUÉ

13, rue Moret 75011 Paris
- Métro: Couronnes
- Information: 01 48 05 96 89
- Wednesday at 20.30, at La Cantada II (October to mid-July)
- www.cantada.net; www.pascaltourain.free.fr
- Admission free; "pass the hat" after the show

Well known to Parisian Goths and fans of heavy metal, the La Cantada II bar, already distinguished by its dizzying range of absinthes, also has a cellar that provides the setting for a show unique in its genre: every Wednesday evening at 20.30, Pascal Tourain tells his own story, that of a man entirely covered by tattoos, except for his face and hands.

"It's permanent, sure, but on something that's only temporary ..."

In the jargon of French tattoo artists, Pascal Tourain is a "bleu", someone who has transformed his body into a veritable tattoo museum, with the help of artist Tin-Tin, revered by all Parisian fans of this corporeal art form.

Throughout his unusual spectacle, Pascal Tourain is both a commentator on tattoos and a human fresco. After cleverly making his audience pine for nearly an hour, he will finally strip off the bathrobe and scarf that entirely cover his body, retaining a G-string as sole garment. At this point you'll discover a lavish work, complete with daft little dramas and illustrations, allusions to the Marquis de Sade sharing space with a detail from a painting by Hieronymus Bosch and reproductions of posters for picturesque fairground characters: a fakir, a human earthworm, Siamese twins, etc. Author, actor, storyteller and teacher all rolled into one, this "tattooed man" has conceived this spectacle to show off his body, to be sure, but also and perhaps most of all in order to help those lacking tattoos to understand better what they're missing. "I'm always being asked why I've done this … But does anyone ask other people why they don't have tattoos? Never!" he fumes. For those who worry about the indelible nature of the marks decorating his skin, he has the ultimate comeback: "It's permanent, sure, but on something that's only temporary!"

If the dumb jokes and rather obvious puns dotting the script of this one-man show sometimes fall flat, the man's sincerity and his great lucidity concerning his choice in life – that of making his body into a work of art – are a delight. It's an astonishing spectacle, both touching and deliberately old-fashioned, halfway between a stand-up comic and a fairground show.

EVENINGS AT LA CANTADA II

There are other appealing concepts to enliven the daily routine at La Cantada II: rock karaoke, divine Sundays (wine-tasting on the first Sunday of the month), apéritifs with short film screenings (second Sunday) and *apéro trock* (you get rid of your books, CDs and DVDs, receiving chits that can be exchanged for objects left by other participants). Off-beat theatre plays and heavy metal concerts are also staged in the room downstairs.

C.O.N.S.O.L.E.

13, rue de la Folie-Régnault 75011 Paris
- Métro: Charonne or Philippe-Auguste
- Contact: Muriel Colin-Barrand
- Tel: 01 43 56 28 22
- E-mail: c.o.n.s.o.l.e@free.fr

C reated in 2001, C.O.N.S.O.L.E. is not just any art gallery but the home of the organizer of this unique contemporary art space. Muriel Colin-Barrand invites visual

Art on site

artists, video-makers and musicians to exhibit, present and perform their works here.

The superb loft, elegantly renovated in the purest "bobo" (bourgeois-bohemian) tradition of the 11th arrondissement, is intended to be a platform for contemporary art in its most diverse forms. Various permanent works by artists form an integral part of the building: a wall painting, pearls embedded in concrete and a sound installation are all there for curious visitors to inspect.

At regular intervals, C.O.N.S.O.L.E. is taken over for "AG glo" weekends, a concept that combines video projections, concerts and showcases with texts and presentations by numerous artists.

This space, defining itself as "a place of exhibition and experimentation", is in constant evolution, in accord with a fluid and fluctuating conception of art, its media and its actors. You are thus invited to subscribe to the news feed on its website in order to keep up to speed on the different forms of exhibition being organized.

© C.o.n.s.o.l.e.

YOGA DU RIRE

Salle de rencontres de la paroisse Sainte-Marguerite
6 bis, rue Jean Macé 75011 Paris • Métro: Charonne
• Tuesday 19.30–20.30
• Information: yogari@club-internet.fr
• http://clubderire.com
•Admission: €5 per session or €15 per month

Besides lymphatic drainage and foot reflexology, the great family of New Age personal development methods includes another odd but enjoyable activity: the yoga of laughter.

Healing laughter

As its name indicates, this involves alternating between breathing exercises and bouts of collective amusement, aimed at stimulating the brain, regulating organic functions, reducing stress, and of course, "laughing together for no reason".

After some classic yoga warm-up exercises, things get serious. Arranged in a circle, the participants all together utter a series of "ha-ha's!" followed by "ho-ho's!" and "hi-hi's!"

"Now you're going to walk across the room, shaking hands and laughing when you hear the name of your partner," orders Chantal, the yoga "laughologist".

"Hello, I'm Sylvie." "Ho-ho, very funny, I'm Jean-Paul, ha-ha-ha …" Not to worry, after a first few minutes of panic, one soon becomes used to this somewhat forced game whose goal, paradoxically, is to provoke spontaneous laughter. At the end of each exercise, the yoga students utter a series of "Ho-ho-ha-ha-ha's" as a sort of rallying cry that serves as a refrain throughout the session.

As the only form of oral expression permitted is laughter, you learn to laugh by imitating in turn a lion, a bear, a motorboat starting up, anger and love.

The high point of the evening, however, comes later, when each participant must present themselves, proudly parading before the others as they chant their name and applaud, laughing loudly all the while.

Lastly, everyone lies down on a floor mat and begins a session of freestyle laughter that lasts a good five minutes, during which all kinds of sonorous excesses are welcome.

All good jokes having a punch line, it's then time for everyone to go back to their normal daily routine.

LE CINÉ-CLUB DES ARTISANS

5, cité de l'Ameublement 75011 Paris
- Métro: Faidherbe-Chaligny
- Friday evening, about twice per quarter
- Admission free (50 persons maximum)

Bring your own chair to a marvellous film club

In contrast to the decidedly soporific and pseudo-intellectual atmosphere of film clubs for readers of Cahiers du cinéma, the Ciné-club des Artisans is resolutely anti-elitist. More than film lovers, above all it tends to draw curious residents from the Nation-Alexandre Dumas neighbourhood.

Since 2004, the local council has been holding these screenings with the help of Patrice, a local mattress-maker. The film club is set up in his vast workshop which is emptied for the occasion. Patrice is an interesting character. A big fan of little-known old movies, he has been organizing these evenings along with Martine, an interested council member. The pair seek out their selections only from collectors: silent films from the beginning of the 20th century, accompanied on the piano by the director of the local music conservatory, and "forgotten junk" from the postwar period are shown alongside contemporary short films by young Parisian directors.

The film club now offers one of the best evenings around and is beginning to attract visitors from beyond the 11th arrondissement. But you need to be motivated and not only bring a bottle or a little snack to share in the interval, but above all, bring your own chair. We advise those who don't live in the 11th to borrow one from a local friend, or else come by car, although a trip by métro with your chair might be a good way to meet people …

SUNDAY CINEMA AT MARLUSSE ET LAPIN
Marlusse & Lapin
14, rue Germain-Pilon 75018 Paris
- Métro: Abbesses or Pigalle
- Screenings every Sunday at 17.00

Every Sunday, in this bar decorated in the manner of a private flat, films are projected behind the bar, on a screen surrounded by an old gilded frame. There is only seating for around twenty. If you enjoy commentary from barflies and impassioned metaphysical debates, stick around after the film. On other days of the week, Jean-Marie, an excellent session guitarist, may show up at any time with his portable amplifier.

TAROT READINGS WITH ALEXANDRO JODOROWSKY

Le Téméraire : 32, avenue Dausmenil 75012 Paris • Métro: Gare de Lyon
• From 18.00 (but turn up anytime after 15.00) on Wednesdays when Jodorowsky is in Paris
• Tel: 01 43 07 56 87

Le Bar sans Nom : 49, rue de Lappe 75011 Paris • Métro: Bastille
• Tuesday from 18.00. First arrivals queue from 16.00 onwards
• Tel: 01 48 05 59 36

O nce a week, Alexandro Jodorowsky conducts some highly unusual proceedings in Le Téméraire café.

For those who've never heard of him before, Master Jodorowsky – known as "Jodo" - is a Chilean of Russian origin who is now aged over 80. A grand provocateur, savant and fringe celebrity, he's best known for his psychedelic bandes dessinées published by Les Humanoïdes Associés, notably his legendary Inkal. But he's also famous for his psychological tarot readings, an approach to self-knowledge that combines the Marseille tarot deck, psychogenealogy and psychoanalysis. Developing a method that is greatly inspired by shamanism, Jodo prescribes "acts" of psycho-magic that are intended to free spirits of their burdens.

A chance to meet Jodorowsky in person

Here are some samples of his recommendations: go for a stroll along the Champs-Élysées wearing nothing but a raincoat and ask passers-by to caress your belly; take deliberately bad photos and give them to your mother; place a bowl of urine beneath your bed for a week …

For the honour and privilege of meeting Jodo, it's best to set aside the whole afternoon … Try to arrive at exactly 15.30. At that time, the owner of bar sells tickets, for around €1, on which each candidate inscribes their name. An hour later there's a draw, and only thirty tickets are selected.

For €4 and the purchase of some drinks at the bar, the winners can await the arrival of Jodorowsky. But even if your name hasn't been picked you can join the crowd of tarot students and other attentive on-lookers, scrutinizing the master's every word and gesture. Encounters with unusual people are guaranteed.

Psychological tarot having a largely female following, those who admire icy Russian beauties or young women students of the paranormal will be satisfied.

If the conditions seem too restrictive, you can always go along to the Bar sans Nom on rue de Lappe, where some of Jodorowsky's students give free readings on Tuesdays. But here again, it's wise to turn up before 17.00 to reserve a place, and also let you get to know the other fortune-telling fans seated around the table.

LA ROULOTTE DU PÈRE-LACHAISE...
ALTIZ, THE TAROT MESSENGER
Caravan opposite 55–65 boulevard Ménilmontant 75011 Paris
• Métro: Père-Lachaise • Advance booking only • www.altiz.com
• Specific questions: €10 per question
• Complete reading (1–1¹/₂ hours): €70

A tarot messenger, to be sure, but also magus of the "forains" (fairground folk) of France and MP for the Republic of Montmartre, Altiz is the proud collector of the most picturesque honorific titles. As the descendant of a long line of fairground stallholders and cartomancers, Altiz claims to be the "last fortune-teller in France". He provides readings by appointment in his caravan, or "professional office", as he makes clear to those who believe he actually lives opposite the Père Lachaise cemetery. The interior of the caravan is very minimalist, without any gypsy décor. "Perhaps I went too far," the man says regretfully. Only a few years ago, he could be seen at French fairgrounds wearing his magus costume!

INVITE A PSYCHIC INTO YOUR LIVING ROOM
EVENING PARANORMAL DEMONSTRATIONS WITH ERICK FEARSON
Evening paranormal demonstrations with Erick Fearson
• Duration of paranormal experiments: 1¹/₂ hours
• From 8 to 20 people: €30 per person, host free of charge
• Erick Fearson will also perform tarot readings in your home
• Tel: 06 70 20 19 33
• www.erickfearson.com

Erick Fearson, who describes himself as a "mentaliste" and "artiste psychique", has achieved notoriety in the press with respect to all things relating to spiritualism and the paranormal. Frequently in demand for investigations of hauntings and television programmes on mysterious phenomena, Fearson has set up a website (www.maison-hantée.com) which gathers together numerous texts and specialist articles.

At the same time, he offers an original concept that appeals greatly to Parisian fans of the supernatural: evening paranormal demonstrations. At first reserved to luxury hotels in the capital with their wealthy celebrity clientele, he now stages these evenings in the homes of common mortals. By your fireplace (if you have one!) or in another setting suitable for summoning strange phenomena, he will entertain your guests by getting them to take part in experiments concerning memory, telepathy, clairvoyance and divination, inspired by the interest in spiritualism fashionable in the 19th century.

If Fearson likes to exaggerate the air of mystery and trepidation surrounding the paranormal, he openly admits that he prefers to organize these evenings in the homes of those who show some scepticism. There is no question here of offering an interpretation that will be taken too literally by the participants or playing with clients' gullibility like some fortune-tellers & All that forms part of a world that Fearson knows well, being the last in a long line of hypnotists, seers and illusionists. In fact, as he frequently says in jest, "For me, the paranormal is completely normal!"

NUDE SWIMMING
AT ROGER LE GALL POOL

Centre nautique Roger Le Gall
34, boulevard Carnot 75012 Paris
• Métro: Porte de Vincennes
• Monday and Wednesday 21.00–23.00, Friday 21.30–23.30
• Identity card required
• Admission: €7 (visitors). Free for under-27s
• Free admission form downloadable from website

Skinny-dipping in Paris

In summer, nudists can leave the capital on family holidays and enjoy the beaches reserved for their use. But what about in winter? It's difficult to practice this particular form of leisure in the heart of Paris, especially when the thermometer reaches its lowest point!

Fortunately for these people (and you?), the Association des Naturistes de Paris (ANP) enjoys use of the Roger Le Gall municipal swimming pool, in the 12th arrondissement, three evenings per week. That's good news for all men (above all!) and women who prefer total nudity. Don't be fooled by the schedule posted at this pool indicating that everything stops at 20.00.

For those who aren't used to nudism, it may be disconcerting, especially when swimmers with goggles seem to be indulging in underwater voyeurism as you pass by …

Note that the people making use of the pool at these hours are 99% male and include a certain number of gay couples. The average age tends towards 40, which explains the financial inducements for younger ages (free admission for under-27s) and "ladies" (a loyalty card offered with membership).

When we asked why male-female parity remained such a distant goal in the urban nudist milieu, we were told, "There still seems to be some reticence here towards nudism." But we should point out that northern Europeans seem to have abandoned such notions of modesty and that in Germany, the Netherlands and Scandinavia, totally nude men and women mix freely in saunas without any apparent embarrassment.

NB: these evenings have absolutely nothing to do with any "swinging" or other sexual activity. Anyone whose words or gestures are deemed sexually "suggestive" will be immediately expelled from the swimming area …

ASSOCIATION NATURISTE DE PARIS
• Tél. : 01 40 30 48 29
• Email : info@naturistes-paris.org
• www.naturistes-paris.org

TOTAL NUDITY IN A MARAIS BAR
L'IMPACT
18, rue Greneta 75002 Paris
- Métro: Châtelet-Les Halles
- Tel: 01 42 21 94 24
- Every evening
- Admission: €11, €6 for under-30s

Much more than just a nudist hang-out, L'Impact is "one of the hottest places in Paris", according to its website Ɛ The concept consists quite simply of casting off your clothes at the entrance, and then walking into a room to meet people, glass in hand and naked as a newborn babe Ɛ In contrast to official nudist evenings (see above), no one here objects to sexual come-ons. For informed gays or heteros who like to be caressed or take risks. Respectful of certain people's sense of modesty, on Thursdays L'Impact organizes a "ProgressivNaked" evening, where you undress little by little ...

EVENING RACES AT THE HIPPODROME DE VINCENNES

2, route de la Ferme 75012 (Bois de Vincennes)
• Métro: Château de Vincennes, then bus 112 to "Carrefour de Beauté" stop;
RER: Joinville-le-Pont (free shuttles)
• Evening races on Tuesday and Friday, 19.45–23.30, from end of March to
beginning of July, and from end of August to beginning of December
• Tel: 01 49 77 17 17 • www.cheval-francais.com
• Customer service (for evening package options): 01 46 99 34 29
• Admission (entry): €3

Rather than simply endure the never-ending PMU racing results on the radio, why not go the full length and discover the peculiar universe of horseracing …

*Plunge
into the universe
of racegoers*

Paris is well-equipped, with the racetracks of Auteuil, Longchamp and Vincennes. The latter, devoted to trotting races, extends its activities into the evening, from early spring to late autumn.

For those not keen on this idea, note that the evening crowd is much more family-friendly and cheerful than during the day …

If the press release can be believed, "From the racetrack's panoramic restaurants, or its private salons, you will enjoy an astounding evening in an unusual setting …" The truth is that there's nothing like getting right into the thick of things, out on the stands or in the immense hall where results are screened non-stop. You'll have more fun there and be able to rub shoulders with real punters, for whom the horses are a passion, a potential source of income … and an addiction!

The racing fanatic, typically an older man, has an expert knowledge of his field, thanks to poring over the specialist press tips, unintelligible to the layman.

Don't be discouraged if you can't make head or tail of it all. Just soak up the old-fashioned "atmosphere" of the Parisian demi-monde here at the racetrack. It's an ideal outing to get away from the stuffy and politically correct tone of more traditional spots.

© Christian RICHARD (Cheval Français)

LES VOÛTES

19, rue des Frigos 75013 Paris
• Métro/RER: Bibliothèque François Mitterrand; Métro: Quai de la Gare
• Go down a short flight of steps, continue towards the right-hand side of the building to the little door leading into the garden
• E-mail: lesvoutes@lesvoutes.org
• www.lesvoutes.org

An alternative venue

Just below the famous Frigos, these four vaults located beneath rue de Tolbiac host all year round concerts, live performances, alternative video screenings, contemporary, noisy and otherwise experimental music, and multimedia spectacles.

Managed by artists from the adjoining Frigos, Les Voûtes welcomes a knowledgeable arty public to its shows, with a bar-restaurant open for these occasions which serves family-style cuisine at unbeatable prices. The association that runs Les Voûtes is also in charge of the surrounding garden, a bucolic spot right in the middle of a concrete and steel neighbourhood, accessible only during the public events (the same applies to the whole site). In a relaxed and rather convivial atmosphere for an arts venue in Paris, you will perhaps have a chance to chat with some of the occupants of the Frigos and see the astonishing interior of this immense arts complex.

LES FRIGOS

A group of refrigerated industrial warehouses built at the beginning of the 20th century, "Les Frigos" were converted in the early 1980s into an artists' residence. The graffiti, the dilapidated goods lifts, and visible plumbing all confer upon this complex the rebellious air of a Berlin squat. But this would be an erroneous impression, since the present occupants have been paying rent to the French railway company (SNCF), for twenty years, and more recently to the municipality of Paris which bought the site.

A hundred visual artists and musicians work daily in this former industrial centre. The tower in the form of a lighthouse rises proudly in the midst of the ultra-modern buildings of the new Paris-Rive-Gauche business district, whose rapid development threatens the continued survival of the place.

Les Frigos has two restaurants. The first, located on the building's "quay", is run by a Japanese resident and offers "Japanese or mixed" cuisine, depending on the day (La Maison des Frigos, Tel: 01 44 23 76 20). The other, the Aiguillage Galerie, is inside the building on the ground floor (see *Secret Bars & Restaurants in Paris* in this series of guides).
www.les-frigos.com

TEMPLE ANTOINISTE

34, rue Vergniaud 75013 Paris
• Métro: Corvisart
• Reading of the Father's teachings, Monday to Friday at 19.00,
Sunday at 10.00
• "Operation" (by means of prayer) in the name of the Father on Sunday
to Thursday at 10.00

The strange little yellow church that stands at the corner of rues Vergniaud and Wurtz, belonging to the Antoinist movement (see below), maintains as a basic tenet its faith in the healing powers of prayer. Inside, a feeling of peace and tranquility reigns and the ambience is straight out of the TV series Little House on the Prairie, with the men in long black frock coats and the women wearing, in addition to black dresses, very 19th-century traditional headdresses.

A curious Belgian faith ...

Silence is strictly observed within the temple, but if you are a believer it is possible to speak, within the "cabinet", in the company of a "healer" who will pray to relieve you of your moral or physical suffering. The battle against pain is one of the pillars of Antoinism, as attested by the title of the Father's most important work, *Délivrez-nous du mal* [Deliver us from evil], on sale at the church.

THE ANTOINIST FAITH

Started in Belgium in 1910, the Antoinist faith (from the name of Antoine, its founder, also called "Father" by its followers) was recognized as a "public service foundation" by the Belgian Government in 1922. It was nevertheless considered to be a faith-healing movement in the 1995 parliamentary report on religious sects, which analysed it in the following terms: "The notion of illness is denied, as is death (belief in reincarnation): it is intelligence that creates suffering, while only faith can suppress it, rather than medical professionals." But followers reject being labelled as a sect, for them their movement is "a moral undertaking based on faith and selflessness & It is a public faith, open to all without distinction or fee". They also point out: "The Father received the sick for twenty-two years. When he started, he had savings allowing him to live without working; when he died, he no longer possessed anything." Today, there are sixty-four Antoinist temples and ninety reading rooms throughout the world, mainly in France, Belgium, Australia and Luxembourg . The faith has about 2,500 followers in France and 200,000 worldwide.

There are two other Antoinist temples in Paris:
10, impasse Roux 75017 Paris • Métro: Ternes or Pereire; RER: Pereire-Levallois
49, rue du Pré Saint-Gervais 75019 Paris • Métro: Pré Saint-Gervais

JIM HAYNES – SUNDAY DINNERS

- Métro: Alésia or Saint-Jacques; RER: Denfert-Rochereau
- To preserve Jim's peace of mind, we leave it to him to send you the address and access code on request
- Sunday at 20.00 • Tel: 01 43 27 17 • www.jim-haynes.com
- Price: €25 ("or less if you're broke")

Jim'll fix it

"Connecting people …" The famous slogan for a brand of telephone has no doubt been borrowed by Jim Haynes, a fairly typical representative of the North American intellectual counter-culture in Paris. His CV, duly noted in detail on his website, gives some idea of his creative hyperactivity: Jim has founded theatres and worked as a writer, editor and teacher, with unceasing energy and boundless joie de vivre. "For me, happiness is an intellectual concept, and I decided years ago to be happy," he explains on his homepage.

A Parisian now for over thirty years, Jim came up with a concept which has since become something of a Franco-American institution: "Sunday Dinners", an unbeatable way of banishing those Sunday evening blues …

On the strength of his enormous popularity, for the past twenty-five years Jim has been organizing these convivial meals gathering together friends, friends of friends, relatives of friends of friends, etc. … in a resolutely party atmosphere. Because at Jim's house, talking to strangers is a social obligation. Perched on his stool and drawing on his formidable memory for people's names, Jim presents you to those around him and then entreats you to chat with any one of them: "Is everyone talking to someone?" he calls out every quarter of an hour. Although perfect for those who want to practise their English live, these evenings should not put off anyone who has difficulty with foreign languages. At these dinners, one finds that about a third of those present are French, while the Americans, mostly expatriate New Yorkers, usually have a good grasp of French. And their desire to strike up a conversation with you tends to increase greatly if you're young and smiling …

Drawing his share of wandering souls from both the artistic milieu and the bone idle, always seeking places to meet new people, the Sunday Dinners also attract a few noteworthy characters connected to Left Bank literary circles. Between the regulars, the originals, and newcomers, you'll be certain to find common ground with the other diners. In summer, the guests move out into the garden next to the studio.

CONCERTS IN A "BABA COOL" CABIN
LE 24 BIS
24 bis, rue Gassendi 75014 Paris
- Métro/RER: Denfert-Rochereau; Métro: Gaité
- Friday and Saturday 18.00–23.00, concert at 21.00
- Tel (Auguste): 06 62 01 40 59 • E-mail: au24bis@hotmail.fr
- www.shokola.com/24bis • Price: €5 (admission + first drink)
- Glass of wine, beer or fruit juice: € 3
Appealing little concerts in a curious cabin backing onto a Parisian building.

u fil

s d'être

Calle
e booth
ows its number
n then, at my leisure,
ne at the other end

e conversations might be recorded;
exclusive use

SOPHIE CALLE'S PHONE BOX

Pont du Garigliano 15th arrondissement
• Tramway: Pont du Garigliano; RER: Boulevard Victor
• The telephone rings five times a week, at random

The numerous Parisians who drive nearby along the embankments or cross the Pont du Garigliano, at the very end of the 15th arrondissement, are probably still wondering what this is.

A phone box unlike any other ...

In the middle of the bridge, the peculiar metallic structure placed on the pavement represents a flower opening its petals. Conceived by the famous architect Frank O. Gehry, who designed the Guggenheim museum in Bilbao, this sculpture also happens to be a phone box.

But if your mobile has just dropped into the Seine below, don't expect to use this box to place a call: the phone box is actually a work of contemporary performance art. Five times a week, the artist Sophie Calle (who launched the project in partnership with Gehry) is thus supposed to call the box at random times. Passers-by are invited to pick up the phone, to take part in an original artistic experience: Sophie Calle will tell you a story and you can then tell her another …

As a matter of fact, she keeps her promise and does indeed call five times a week. Some conversations between the artist and passers-by have lasted more than an hour.

For an unusual and enjoyable evening, you can thus stand by the phone box and wait for her call. Statistically, it should happen within two days … One major benefit: since the calls are recorded for probable future artistic use, you'll thus have the immense privilege of becoming an artist in your own right.

THE T3 LINE, AN ASTONISHING OPEN-AIR MUSEUM

Impelled by the laudable aim of making passengers' journeys on the Maréchaux Sud tramway more enjoyable, the Paris city council commissioned nine contemporary artworks to be placed as landmarks along the line. Besides Sophie Calle's phone box, one of the most surprising of these works is probably the sound installation set up by Christian Boltanski in Parc Montsouris. Ten park benches are fitted with speakers emitting confessions of love in foreign languages. This is a wink at the nearby Cité Universitaire Internationale, since these amorous murmurings were recorded by foreign students living in Paris.

Another intriguing creation is Mirage by Bertrand Lavier, an ensemble of fake palm trees that emerge once every hour at random intervals behind the Poterne des Peupliers (a fortified city gate dating from the 19th century) …

LOGE UNIE DES THÉOSOPHES

11 bis, rue Kepler 75116 Paris
- Métro: George V, Kléber or Étoile
- Lectures Friday at 20.15 and on the first Sunday of the month at 17.30
- Tel: 01 47 20 42 87 • www.theosophie.asso.fr
- E-mail: theosophie@theosophie.asso.fr

O pposite the Libyan Embassy, rue Kepler is home to the intriguing Loge Unie des Théosophes. Theosophical concepts and literature are so abundant that members themselves have difficulty providing a comprehensible synthesis. The best thing is to go there and find out for yourself: the lectures are free and curious enquirers are welcome.

Delving into the secrets of the Great Architect

The lodge (nothing to do with freemasonry) organizes its debates in a vast hall graced by a library in carved wood, a fanciful setting worthy of a Roman Polanski film or a Dan Brown novel.

After an hour's presentation of some aspect of theosophy, the sessions are thrown open to questions from the public. You then discover that the audience is not composed solely of regulars haunting the esoteric milieux of Paris: attracted by theosophy's humanist principles and its openness to sacred texts of all origins, mathematicians, physicists and philosophers often show up for these talks.

SOCIÉTÉ THÉOSOPHIQUE DE FRANCE

4, square Rapp 75007 Paris • RER: Pont de l'Alma
- Lectures open to the public on Sunday afternoon at around 16.00
- Tel: 01 47 05 26 30 • Bookshop: 01 45 51 31 79
- www.theosophie-adyar.com

The Société Théosophique is the other theosophical institution in Paris. Housed in a superb, specially constructed building, the society has a bookshop open on Wednesday and Thursday (10.00–18.00), and Friday and Saturday (12.00–18.00), as well as a library, both devoted to theosophical topics. Calling its rival on rue Kepler a "dissident" branch, the society regards itself as more open, notably offering the teachings of Krishnamurti (1895–1986), the famous Indian thinker and for a time member of theosophical circles, who consider him to be a "world instructor".

THEOSOPHY

The Theosophical Society, founded in the 19th century by Helena Petrovna Blavatsky, an international traveller, draws its principles from Plato, Christianity, Buddhism and Hinduism. In its attempt to create a universal brotherhood of humanity, theosophy has inspired such artists as Kandinsky, Mondrian, Kafka and Pollock. Disrupted in its later development by disagreements among the founder's successors, the society has largely been forgotten today, although members maintain the faith in Los Angeles, Athens and London. Gandhi paid homage to theosophy, however, and the theoreticians of the New Age movement have been heavily influenced by its teachings.

BAHÁ'Í WEDNESDAY TALKS

Centre Bahá'í
45, rue Pergolèse 75116 Paris
• Métro: Argentine or Porte Maillot
• Tel: 01 45 00 90 26 • www.bahai.fr
• Wednesday from 19.45, admission free
• Informal talk and discussion from 20.00 to 21.30

Discover the Bahá'í faith

Totally unknown to the French general public, the Bahá'í faith has almost 6 million members worldwide. But the Bahá'í do no preaching and are happy to receive curious visitors at their centre in the 16th arrondissement, rue Pergolèse.

The Bahá'í weekly informal talks take place in a vast salon on the ground floor of the affluent-looking building that houses their French headquarters. To the sound of New Age music, non-initiates are invited to listen to the history of this religion originating in Persia and to ask any questions they might have. After a few exchanges among participants, a moment of "interreligious prayer" is called for, during which everyone reads a passage from the texts of Bahá'u'lláh, founder of the faith. No prior knowledge is required to participate, it is enough to be patient and to enjoy contemplative literature. Without being active proselytizers, the Bahá'ís are nevertheless impressive due to the strength of their faith and unfailing bliss in all circumstances … some rather strange souls may be your prayer companions.

The Bahá'í adepts are remarkably well organized and bestow numbers with a strong symbolic meaning: elections held every five years allow them to choose nine local representatives, who vote for the nine members of national assemblies, charged in turn with selecting the nine members of the Universal House of Justice, the Bahá'í faith's world headquarters in Haifa, Israel. The Bahá'ís also use a calendar composed of nineteen months of nineteen days each.

BAHÁ'Í FAITH

Founded in Iran in the 19th century by Mirzá Husayn 'Alî, the Bahá'í faith takes its name from Bahá'u'lláh (Arabic: "Splendour of God"), as he was known. A syncretism stemming from Bábism (a reformist Shi'ite movement which put forward a new definition of the prophets), this faith draws its sources from Islam, but also other revealed religions. Persecuted in Iran since the very beginning of their spiritual movement, the Bahá'ís have nevertheless spread throughout the world: Bahá'u'lláh's eldest son, Abbas Effendi, travelled to Europe and the United States, and succeeded in exporting the faith.

The movement, recognized as a non-governmental organization by the United Nations, assists in economic and social development through a variety of local projects, as well as fostering dialogue between different peoples and religions. They believe in universal values such as education, the unity of humanity, equality between the sexes, economic justice and, of course, world peace.

ARTS D'AUSTRALIE APARTMENT-GALLERY
– STÉPHANE JACOB

- Métro: Pereire
- Evening presentations of the collection, twice weekly, by appointment only
- Information and reservations: 01 46 22 23 20
- E-mail: sj@artsdaustralie.com
- www.artsdaustralie.com

Stéphane Jacob, a renowned expert on Australian art, organizing numerous exhibitions and providing pieces to the most prestigious museums, holds in his storeroom the canvases of some of the most sought-after contemporary artists, but also a host

Australian art in a Parisian living room

of traditional aboriginal objects: shields, boomerangs, and even a knife used in the circumcision of young adults. For a decade now, he has invited art lovers to come and discover his treasures in the intimate and unusual setting of his flat.

With a map of Australia as a guide and a highly infectious enthusiasm for his subject, the gallery owner parades his pieces, manipulates them every which way, and then cordially invites visitors to do the same. The original concept of presenting them in an apartment takes away some of the sacredness of the works and encourages participants to ask all manner of questions and, of course, discuss money matters more freely. The gallery owner has no qualms about evoking the financial side of things, and that's all to the good. And don't be afraid of being held ransom in his home – at the end of his talk, Stéphane Jacob announces, "Now you can run along if you wish!"

The set-up seems to be an outright success, as thanks to word-of-mouth and some media coverage, the Jacobs, mother and son, welcome a dozen people twice a week: collectors and wealthy amateurs, but also students and people curious to learn more about Australian culture.

VIVRASIE – ANTIQUE FURNITURE AND RARE OBJECTS FROM ASIA
85, boulevard Malesherbes 75008 Paris
- Métro: Villiers, Europe or Saint-Augustin
- Open until 22.00 by prior appointment with Aline Pintaud
- Tel: 01 55 30 00 06 • E-mail: aline.pintaud@vivrasie.com

Located on the first floor of a building in the 8th arrondissement, Aline Pintaud's gallery has some superb Asian works of art and furniture. Although private visits can be booked, exhibition launches and open days also take place throughout the year. "For those who are shy about making an appointment," the gallery owner stresses. She welcomes all her visitors in a friendly and personalized manner, and that is exactly what seems to appeal to her clients, who pass on her address while others wear themselves out shopping along boulevard Haussmann on Saturday afternoons. Several times a year, Aline goes off to Asia to renew her stock. She can thus bring back for you that Buddha or gong you've always been dreaming of, if you put in your request before she goes.

LA NUIT ÉLASTIQUE

- Dress code (minimum): leather, vinyl or latex pants or skirt
- http://www.nuit-elastique.com
- Ticket advance sales: €15 to €30

(Demonia boutique, 10 cité Joly 75011 Paris, Tel: 01 43 14 82 70)

L a Nuit Élastique is probably the most stupefying evening listed in this guide. According to the official terminology, it is "an evening aimed at all fetishists of leather, vinyl or latex". Open to the public on the condition of wearing, at least, pants or a skirt made from one of these three materials, the evening is organized with the Demonia boutique, a platform for the "BDSM" (bondage, dominance, sadomasochism) community in Paris, and brings together several hundred people each month.

The biggest fetishist evening in Paris

Less hardcore readers may want to content themselves with a daytime visit to the Demonia boutique, which is also definitely worth a look.

The evening's ambience soon makes itself felt: once inside, you'll encounter men and women who are practically naked, others who are almost completely wrapped in leather or latex, while men sporting YMCA moustaches stand side-by-side with manga heroines and young trendy Goths. At the bar, a man lying on the ground has his torso crushed under the boot of a creature who is visibly very angry with him …

Once your nerves settle from the impression of having walked into a Marilyn Manson video, and after some warming-up on the dance floor, which is rather mainstream in its selection of heavy metal and Goth tracks, it's time to get down to serious business … In the back room, modestly hidden from the rest of the basement space by a black curtain that can be penetrated by anyone, the dress code is relatively clear. Fitted with collars that you can attach a chain or leash to, slaves quietly await the arrival of their mistresses. These, whip in hand, moulded and cinched into accessories that tend towards the military, indulge in S&M games that range from "simple" bootlicking to less innocent practices where martinets expertly crack whips across the round bottoms of their willing victims.

We hasten to point out that we aren't sending you to the slaughter: these dealings only involve consenting adults, and in principle you won't be obliged to take part. Most of the time you'll be left alone in a corner while you satisfy your curiosity, and at best (or worst?) a young transvestite will come for a friendly word and in a surreal fashion offer to be your personal slave for the evening or perhaps even longer …

LA MAIZON

13, rue Collette 75017 Paris
Ground floor, left-hand door
• Métro: Guy Môquet
• Monday to Friday 19.00–23.00, Saturday 16.00–23.00, Sunday
16.00–19.00
• Tel: 01 42 26 33 36
• www.lamaizon.net

"Houze"
of happiness

Although Anouk originally wanted to leave the Épinettes neighbourhood, which she found to be rather banal and impersonal, she finally told herself that with a little imagination and plenty of energy, she could make this corner of Paris a haven of conviviality and solidarity. And that's how, in September 2004, the idea of La Maizon was born.

Not really a house at all, the place is in fact a 60 m² apartment on the ground floor of a building facing the square des Épinettes.

Various volunteers, having met through the Peuplade community website and around the neighbourhood, gradually converged on Anouk's project to convert the premises into a proper "house", a warm and welcoming venue where people would truly feel at home.

The activities have become more numerous and varied as proposals are received from new members: exotic gastronomic meals, language and theatre classes, job-seeking workshops, games evenings, a film club … or quite simply an evening spent in one another's company. Above all, La Maizon is designed for those who, in Paris, are feeling lonely. The unemployed, singles, foreigners … those who visit here are seeking friendship in a city often cruel to its most fragile residents.

Be that as it may, La Maizon is also an appealing place for all different types of people, and is not simply a "lonely-hearts club". With hard-to-beat prices – €6 for a complete meal with a drink – it's also an excellent alternative to a restaurant, bar, or an evening alone with a TV dinner!

Today, Anouk says she feels much better about her neighbourhood, and she only has to lift the phone when she needs a favour. This spirit of neighbourly exchange is very lively at La Maizon, starting with the post-it notes everyone, proposing anything from a place to rent to an opinion of the latest book someone has read …

With a total of thirty-five volunteers, of whom two are present on any given evening, the welcome frequently changes face. But all are here to promote exchanges between members. "Exchange doesn't mean a dating service!" warns the boss. "Although our first couple has officially been formed!" she adds.

MADRAS. INDIA.

V. E. L.

TOUS

MARCH 1868.

TOUT

B

N.D. DES VICTOIRES
1875.
B
O MARIA INNACULÉE

NIGHT OF ADORATION AT SACRÉ-CŒUR

Basilique du Sacré-Cœur
35, rue du Chevalier de la Barre 75018 Paris
• Métro: Anvers, Abbesses or Lamarck-Caulaincourt
• Nuit d'Adoration, every evening from 23.00 to 7.00 (midnight to 7.00 the first Friday of the month)• Registration required at least 24 hours in advance for the Nuit d'Adoration • "Open-door" worship until midnight, on the first Friday of the month, 20.30–24.00
• Tel: 01 53 41 89 00 • www.sacre-coeur-montmartre.com
• Admission: €5 for use of dormitory

Everyone has visited Sacré-Cœur in Montmartre during the daytime, but there are relatively few who can boast of having spent the night within the world-famous basilica on its mound overlooking the capital.

An entire night in Sacré-Cœur

But that's the idea behind the Nuit d'Adoration, a prayer session that lasts from 23.00 until 7 in the morning and will surely move those who haven't lost all sense of spirituality. The reception of worshippers and assignment of places in the dormitory takes place at 20.30. From 21.00 to 23.00, prayers are said in the presence of ordinary visitors. Then the basilica doors are closed, and the worshippers who have signed up beforehand take turns in saying uninterrupted prayers: to be allowed to remain within the church throughout the night, you must agree to stay awake and pray for at least one hour until replaced by another worshipper.

Once your adorational duty has been fulfilled, you can rest in the Sacré-Cœur dormitory. You will thus take part in a great spiritual tradition, since the basilica's perpetual prayer of Adoration has continued without a break, day and night, since 1 August 1885.

AN "OPEN-DOOR" ADORATION NIGHT

You can take part in the Adoration without spending the entire night, each first Friday of the month, when an "open-door" Adoration Night is held. After the evening prayer session led by the Benedictine monks of the Sacré-Cœur of Montmartre at 21.00, the first Adoration prayer takes place from 23.00 to midnight, in which everyone can take part without registering. After that, only the volunteers remain until the early morning to worship the Lord in silence.

LOVE SEATS AT THE CINÉ 13 THEATRE

1, avenue Junot 75018
- Métro: Lamarck-Caulaincourt or Abbesses
- Open from Wednesday to Saturday
- Reservations: 01 42 54 15 12 • www.cine13-theatre.com
- Admission: €25 / €15

Watching a play on a sofa for two

Located in one of the most picturesque spots in Montmartre, and therefore in all of Paris, the Ciné 13 Theatre has some magnificent leather sofas designed to accommodate couples … Although the idea is romantic, we hasten to add that the extraordinary comfort of these sofas frees you from any physical distractions to concentrate on the play itself.

This hall was built by Claude Lelouch, who originally used it as the set for his film *Édith et Marcel*, and later converted into a cinema. Today, it's a theatre with 120 seats, whose programme is devised by Salomé Lelouch, the daughter of the French director.

The theatre also has individual seating which as just as comfortable as the sofas. This arrangement was conceived for the audience of the *Recto/Verso* TV show, which was recorded here. The show is no longer on the air, but the seats and sofas remain.

OTHER LOVE SEATS AT MK2

Following the example of Ciné 13 in Montmartre, the MK2 cinema chain has equipped some of its screening rooms with seating for couples. These "love seats", dreamed up by designer Martin Szekely, will no doubt smooth the advances of novice make-out artists and will please steady couples. In our experience, these seats are the only comfortable way for a couple to watch a film while cuddling.

Cinéma MK2 Bibliothèque
128–162, avenue de France 75013 Paris
- Métro: Bibliothèque François Mitterrand

Cinéma MK2 Quai de Loire
7, quai de la Loire 75019
- Métro: Stalingrad or Jaurès
- Reservations: 08 92 69 84 84

THE BOX IN PARIS

Late-night meals, evening tastings, and buffet-style aperitifs at The Box in Paris gallery
Open Tues-Sat 3pm-8pm, and evenings when events are scheduled
6, cité du Midi, 75018 Paris • Access: Métro Pigalle
• Tel.: 01 42 51 52 42 • E-mail: contact@theboxinparis.com
• Programme: www.theboxinparis.com • Prices: Late-night meal: main dish €15; evening tastings: €35, excluding drinks
• Guest room: bed and breakfast from €150

Various exhibition and living spaces are organised around a big box, hence the name: The Flavour Box, the kitchen, The Lab, the exhibition hall in the basement, as well as The White Box and The Black Box, two very beautiful guest rooms. As for Aline, simultaneously owner, gallery director, cook, and events organizer for this venue, she lives and works in her own separate quarters… The Private Box.

Dinner in a modern art loft-gallery

If the "concept" strikes you as a little pompous at first, don't be misled. Because this large and somewhat austere-looking loft turns out to be a warm and surprising place.

The originality of The Box lies in the proliferation of its nocturnal activities. Organised around photo exhibitions, the gallery comes to life with small concerts, readings, and gastronomic evenings. A sort of 21st-century dining hall, or a "rock 'n' roll" kind of place, as Aline puts it, where you find yourself opening up to total strangers with whom you have been merrily seated at the table.

The menu and the programming changes frequently but the spirit remains the same: somewhere between an arty meeting place and a neighbourhood cultural centre. If the dinners may seem a little expensive to some (€35), the originality and quality of an evening spent here make it well worth the price.

ICE BAR AT HÔTEL KUBE

1–5, passage Ruelle 75018 Paris
• Métro: La Chapelle
• Every evening; advance booking required
• Reservations: 01 42 05 20 00 • E-mail: paris@kubehotel.com
• www.kubehotel.com
• Admission: €38 for a half-hour session with open bar • Rooms: single
€250, double €300

Of course, this isn't the Ice Bar at the Ice Hotel in Swedish Lapland, right up near the Arctic Circle. But the idea is the same and it turns out that you can have a good time here, even if the place has become part of the trendy circuit in the French capital.

Breaking the ice at 5 below zero

Here's the set-up. First of all, you need to be motivated to venture into this rather dreary corner of the 18th arrondissement. Located near the Marx Dormoy métro station, between the railway lines running into the Gare de l'Est and the Gare du Nord, the least one can say is that the Ice Kube is a pioneer. Our advice is to avoid going there on foot, as it might be a rather scary experience ...

The first glimpse is surprising: facing onto a cul-de-sac, a handsome U-shaped building contains the hotel, bar and restaurant. With its designer decor, the restaurant offers a very inventive and rather successful menu. But the really interesting part is upstairs, at the Ice Bar. Book your entry time in advance (the bar's capacity is relatively limited), pay the €38 admission fee, put on the polar suit that is kindly provided, and you're now ready to penetrate into a space maintained at a constant temperature of –5°. With its bar made from ice, snow-covered floor, and ice walls, only the ceiling (sadly) is out of keeping with this arctic setting. Even the glasses are carved from ice,

with the rather startling result that your glass slowly begins to melt as it comes into contact with your burning lips ...

The admission fee gives you the right to drink, for the first 30 minutes, as much as you like of a large variety of vodkas ... In the commendable spirit of turning the cost of the evening to best advantage, it's common practice for customers to down several shots of vodka in 5–10 minutes. Needless to say, the atmosphere soon becomes quite jovial. When you leave, try to sober up a little before wandering off into the neighbourhood ...

SQUAT LA MIROITERIE

88, rue de Ménilmontant 75020 Paris
- Métro: Ménilmontant or Pelleport
- Concerts most weekends and sometimes on weekdays
- Times listed in *Lylo* magazine

A former mirror factory converted for artists' use, La Miroiterie has kept its original name. It offer an irregular programme of rock concerts, with a definite leaning towards punk rock (heavy on guitars with powerful drum backing) and happily maintaining an alternative spirit that its neighbour, La Maroquinerie, has long since lost.

A real rockers' squat

The Miroiterie is a squat that has been occupied for the past six years. Constructed along an alley scattered with old sofas left out in the open air, the buildings provide shelter for about twenty artists who work there, and for the most part, also live there. On the walls behind the refreshment stand are mosaics composed of small bits of mirror providing a reminder of the site's original vocation.

If the recycled furnishings, beer cans, and somewhat sloppy hygiene of the toilets don't put you off, you can watch a concert here in a small, smoke-filled concrete hall, with absolutely terrible acoustics. Even hardcore music fans should bring earplugs: it's no coincidence that the organizers prefer the refreshment stand when the music is playing …

As in the case of most Parisian squats, there's no real planning of activities, so try to call up beforehand or drop by at the right moment. Most invited musicians mobilize their own fans to fill the hall. It's an excellent opportunity, by the way, to observe a transatlantic student crowd come to hear some obscure New York band touring France …

MUSIC LESSONS FROM JEAN-FRANÇOIS ZYGEL

6, place Gambetta 75020 Paris
• Métro: Gambetta
• One Thursday every month, from November to June, at 14.00, 17.00 and 20.00, in the wedding hall at the 20th arrondissement mairie
• Information: Tel: 01 43 15 20 79
• E-mail: parisculture20@wanadoo.fr • www.mairie20.paris.fr
• Admission: €10 • Annual subscription (8 sessions): €50

A music lesson at the town hall

Among the abundant programmes of cultural activities offered by the *mairies d'arrondissement* (Paris town halls), Thursdays in the 20th *arrondissement* stand out due to their popularity with Parisians. Once a month, Jean-François Zygel gives a very popular music lesson.

Zygel is a star of the classical music world: a composer and professor, he also presents TV and radio shows. His originality stems from his prodigious qualities as a teacher and his love of music such that he feels a need to spread it to the masses. More than two hundred fans cram themselves into the wedding hall at the mairie to attend this monthly ritual.

The music lesson is more a one-man show than a standard lecture on the subject. The waltz, the polka and the minuet are demystified in admirable fashion in classes aimed at both knowledgeable music lovers and novices, and in which humour has a prominent place.

Thus, Zygel does not hesitate to interrupt his flow by suddenly plunging into variations on the theme of mobile phone ringtones, provoking laughter from the audience and inflicting shame on the unfortunate culprit who has left theirs switched on.

With his inimitable style, at times precious or even a little bawdy, Zygel is the favourite of musicology students and groups of pensioners alike, who do not hesitate to cross Paris to see the master play. A really good show, and cheap at the price.

A MUSICIAN ACTIVE ON ALL FRONTS

Pianist and composer Jean-François Zygel is professor of composition and improvisation at the Conservatoire National Supérieur de Paris. The popularity of the music lessons he has been giving for the past ten years at the 20th *arrondissement* town hall has led to a radio programme on France Musique, a TV show on France 2 and various DVDs. He was among the Victoire de la Musique Classique winners in 2006, and also gives music lessons at the Théâtre du Châtelet.

THÉÂTRE L'OGRESSE

4, rue des Prairies – corner of 125, rue de Bagnolet 75020 Paris
• Métro: Porte de Bagnolet or Gambetta
• Tel: 01 46 36 95 15
• Programme: www.ogresse.org, or see theatre listings in L'Officiel des spectacles and concerts in Lylo
• Admission: €5 to €8, free for some concerts
• Meals: €8 to €13 • Beer: €3

Alternative puppetry and experimental music

Standing at the corner of two streets, and hidden behind Charonne church, L'Ogresse has two official addresses, as if the place was located between two worlds. And that's also the impression you get after an evening spent in this surprising venue, which is a puppet theatre, a concert hall, a corner bar and a meeting-place all rolled into one. "There are plenty of places in Paris that are alternative on the outside, but turn out to be hollow within; L'Ogresse is alternative through and through," as one regular put it.

Don't be put off if Mutata, the manager of the theatre and also director, puppet master and experimental singer/musician sometimes seems to be missing the point in answering you. His apparent air of distraction disguises a strong and creative spirit: he and his friends are the organizers of these evenings at L'Ogresse.

Here, everyone knows one another and word-of-mouth functions well enough to fill the few dozen seats available in the small theatre. People are on familiar terms and half the audience has free invitations or concessions.

You can also eat here before or after the shows, especially when Mutata has decided the time is right … The same applies to the times of shows: they start when the boss is ready. Before the curtain rises, people chat, some begin to sing … A young woman seen leaving a salsa class a few doors down from the theatre is hailed by the spectators and soon joins the group. Nothing seems to stay fixed or unchanging in this place where people come and go as they please under the benevolent eye of the organizer, who proclaims in his prologue: "You are about to witness a puppet show. Good luck. You can leave whenever you like, the door's over there!"

The puppet show is an ode to improvisation: surrounded by cameras, screens, wires and consoles, Mutata runs the show from A to Z. One unusual feature is that the director encourages the spectators to come backstage if they wish to watch how the puppets are put through their moves.

The second part of the evening takes place in the basement, the space given over to concerts. A word of advice: choose an evening when MKDN, L'Ogresse's house band, is playing. Mutata sings, accompanied by two basses and horns and freely improvising, playing on the innards of a piano that he has taken apart himself! It's experimental music that is disconcertingly surreal, just like this very appealing little theatre.

CONTEMPORARY ART TOUR
AND "STYLEDESIGNARTFOODSEXEBIZARRE" WITH ART PROCESS

• Dining with ...: dinner in the company of leading figures in the arts, once a month at 20.00 • The Art Bus (contemporary art shuttle): third Saturday of the month at 11.00 • The Buzz Bus (graphic arts, design, fashion): first Saturday of the month at 11.00 • Information and reservations: Tel: 01 47 00 90 85
• E-mail: info@art-process.com • www.art-process.com
• Prices: Dining with ..., The Art Bus and The Buzz Bus: €35 (members) and €60 (non-members)• Nocturnal tours à la carte: around 1,200 for a group of 10

A movable feast of contemporary art

"Everything you ever wanted to know about contemporary art but were afraid to ask". That just about sums up the idea behind Art Process, a facility set up by arts experts, somewhere between a style bureau and an events agency. As is well known, contemporary art tends to scare people off. Incomprehensible and elitist ... it's difficult to enter the Paris-New York-(Palais de) Tokyo microcosm formed by creators currently working in the arts. Art Process has set itself the task of identifying the key trends, places and people in this milieu, so that a wider audience of both novice and knowledgeable art lovers can enjoy new work.

A range of cultural activities are on offer. Dining with ..., organized once a month, takes place in a museum or art gallery (see Secret Bars & Restaurants in Paris in this series of guides) and revolves around a specific artistic theme. You have a meal, of course, but above all, you have a chance to meet the experts who speak at these dinner-lectures, designed to accompany a contemporary art exhibition or salon.

Even more unusual – and more expensive – is a night-time tour that can be tailored to the specific needs of a group looking for an original cultural outing. Starting at the centre of Paris, the tour sets out in an American limousine stocked with champagne. During our last visit, the excursion commenced with the galleries in the Marais neighbourhood and ended up in the suburb of Saint-Ouen, after a halt in the 18th arrondissement.

The itineraries generally include five or six stops in "zones of creative turbulence", meaning the places where things are happening.

The programme is both eclectic and cutting-edge, including photo, video, body-work and multimedia projects in real time ...

Normally at a loss in world where they haven't mastered the codes or taken aback by the apparent incongruity of certain works, visitors can rely here on the expertise of their guides and receive a full explanation often lacking when venturing alone into contemporary exhibitions.

CRASHING CELEBRITY PARTIES WITH THE SYNDICAT DU HYPE
Marais and Saint-Germain-des-Près, 7th, 8th, 15th and 16th
arrondissements • Every evening • Admission: free with open bar if you
manage to get in • Agenda and information: www.syndicatduhype.com
or www.vodkacoca.com

As a nerve centre of fashion, art, media and showbiz, Paris is full of merci-
lessly exclusive parties which you can nevertheless join. In order to pass
through the gates with their professional watchdogs, audacity is your main
trump card. You might pluck up courage once you realize that two-thirds of
the people at these gatherings have no business being there, either! These
nocturnal "gate-crashers" have two main reasons for wanting to hang out
at these trendy evenings: the buffet and the various celebrities present.

Art galleries
A promising first avenue available to lovers of luxurious open bars is provided by art show openings. Usually free and open to all, they are full of
scroungers who shamelessly mix with the official guests. Fashionable
dress and a visibly relaxed attitude will help you penetrate this world without arousing suspicion.

Product launches
After the arts world, marketing is also a great supplier of petits fours and
champagne. To launch a new car, line of clothing, or the latest technologi-
cal gadget, communications teams never fail to rent a prestigious venue in
the French capital and invite all those they imagine to be shapers of public
opinion. If you haven't made the guest list, the game consists in keeping
abreast of future events on a daily basis, and show up at the door for the
occasion. To find out about such parties, the internet forum of the Syndicat
du Hype is a very effective research tool. Day after day, it provides reliable
intelligence on forthcoming society gatherings – you'll even find copies of
invitations and fliers that you can print out!
The ultimate nose-thumbing for professional gate-crashers is to be photo-
graphed behind a star and then appear in the following week's issue of *Gala*
or *Voici* magazine ...

Embassies
Ah ... the famous evenings hosted by the ambassador! Who hasn't dreamed
of being one of the happy few to enjoy the tasteful hospitality of a foreign
mission in Paris? Access poses a problem, however, as these evenings are
normally by invitation only. But here again, it is possible to slip under the
radar of those on guard. The Syndicat du Hype website will again prove to
be invaluable in keeping track of the agenda of diplomatic parties.
Once you arrive, there are two possibilities. The first stratagem is relatively risky: don an impeccable outfit and stand in the queue, hoping that
the "spotter" on duty won't admit that they don't recognize an obvious di-
gnitary such as yourself ... Failing that, resort to the much-used password,
"I'm a journalist". Experience shows that you have one chance in three of
getting in.

SOIRÉE DE STAR

- Tel: 01 47 49 80 77
- www.soireedestar.fr
- Price varies: from €289 to €3,469

Soirée de Star would be a perfect gift idea for one of your more flamboyant friends.

The company that launched the idea at the beginning of 2005 offers ordinary Parisians a chance to enjoy their fifteen minutes of fame.

Enjoy your fifteen minutes of fame

In the light of the success of Star Academy and its ephemeral cast, this small narcissistic pleasure seems certain to be a hit with some people.

In an exchange for a rather hefty sum, the events agency plans an evening right down to the smallest detail that will plunge you into the role of a true celebrity.

It starts when two bodyguards show up in a limousine and ring your doorbell in the early evening. They whisk you off in this vehicle with tinted windows, worthy of Madonna descending on the Champs-Élysées, and take you to one of the hyper-selective clubs and restaurants with which the company has arranged priority access. Along the way, actors play the role of hysterical fans, trying to slip past your bodyguards to beg an autograph, or that of a paparazzi following on a motorbike in an attempt to snap a picture of your august self.

On reaching the venue, you are welcomed by a television crew to whom you have already granted the privilege of an exclusive interview.

For purists, Soirée de Star also sets up some other nice finishing touches: an assault on a bodyguard by a crazed fan, who is then masterfully subdued … The package can also be enhanced by an afternoon's makeover, followed by a photo session in the room of a luxury hotel. After having experienced close up the daily life of real stars, who are subjected to this diabolical pace all year round, reading *Voici* will never be quite the same …

© Soirée de star

RADIO RECORDING SESSIONS:
« LA BANDE PASSANTE »

Held alternatively at La Flèche d'Or, La Bellevilloise or Le Triptyque
• To attend these recording sessions, invitations must be picked up,
either in the main hall of La Maison de la Radio, a week in advance
(01 44 30 83 32), or at the recording venues:
• Le Triptyque, 19, rue du Croissant 75002
• La Flèche d'Or, 102 bis, rue de Bagnolet 75020
• La Bellevilloise, 19, rue Boyer 75020
• http://www.rfi.fr/radiofr/emissions/072/accueil-33.asp
• Website for Radio France programmes: http://www.radiofrance.
fr/rf/cparf/emission/
• Attention: closed temporarily. Reopening soon

*Watch
stars in concert
discreetly
and for free*

Mainly composed of regulars who have found ways to do things cheaply in *Paris pas cher*, the audience who turn up for the TV and radio recording sessions move in their own separate world. Whereas most people queue and pay large sums to see their favourite artist perform, these people manage to watch all kinds of cultural events without spending a cent!

Number one among these little-known freebies is RFI's weekly music programme, La Bande Passante, with three invited musicians playing half an hour each, interspersed with interviews by presenter Alain Pilot.

In addition to attending a concert at a trendy venue (La Flèche d'Or, La Bellevilloise or Le Tripyque), the recording sessions for La Bande Passante spare its live audience any laborious preparations, warm-up applause, or hours of waiting that usually ensue when taping a TV show.

The first part of the programme features new French talent and is followed by a headline act: Renaud, Mickey 3D, Vincent Delerm and Brigitte Fontaine have all notably appeared on the show.

Radio France also offers recording sessions for other music programmes at La Maison de la Radio, to which invitations must be collected an hour in advance.

LE MULTICOLORE: PARISIAN ROULETTE

Cercle central :
2, rue Frochot 75009 Paris • Métro: Pigalle
• Tel: 01 42 85 28 45 • Open daily 15.00–6.00
Cercle Clichy-Montmartre :
84, rue de Clichy 75009 • Métro: Place de Clichy
• Tel: 01 48 78 32 85 • Open daily 16.00–6.00
Cercle Wagram :
47, avenue de Wagram 75017 Paris • Métro: Ternes
• 01 43 80 65 13 • Open daily 15.00–6.00

A shady world

Contrary to popular belief, you can play for money in Paris (see box below): although full-fledged casinos are illegal (so those hooked on gambling go to Enghien-les-Bains or Deauville), the French capital has managed to preserve a few out-of-the-way places where a shady crowd departs regularly on their journey to the depths of night.

The atmosphere is a far cry from that of James Bond playing with Eva Green at his side, but these places are still worth a visit: a mix of Chinese (it's no coincidence that Macao has recently dethroned Las Vegas as the world's gambling capital), Pakistanis, Parisian riffraff, their suburban cousins, and a few upper-crust types. It's not at all unusual to see some characters fast asleep in the armchairs around the multicolore table.

"Multi", as regulars call the game, is a simplified form of roulette with four colours. Invented in the 19th century, it is no longer played anywhere outside Paris. The principle is very like roulette, other than that the "banker" launches the ball with the help of a billiard cue. Bets run from €2 to €200, and winnings are multiplied by two, three or four, if you've picked the right colour, or by 24 if you've bet on the star …

In contrast to the often louche crowd, the liveried croupiers deliver, with military precision, chips to the small players and €100 "plaques" to more serious punters.

The banker sits between throws of the ball, placidly watching the constantly renewed struggle between humanity and the laws of chance, while statistics on the latest results flash up on screens.

WHY ARE SOME BETTING GAMES ALLOWED IN PARIS?

French legislation distinguishes between *"jeux de cercle"* (club games) and *"jeux de contrepartie"* (banking games). In jeux de cercle such as *multicolore* or baccarat, the customers are betting against other customers. In casino games such as roulette, boule or blackjack, however, players are competing directly with the house: these are jeux de contrepartie. Only casinos may host such games, in addition to automatic gaming machines. But unlike casinos, banned in Paris, private gaming clubs are authorized to set up shop in the capital.

"DEUX-CHEVAUX" RIDES AROUND PARIS
WITH *4 ROUES SOUS 1 PARAPLUIE*

- Starts and finishes in city centre (1st to 9th arrondissements) or by Opéra Garnier steps
- Information and reservations: 0 800 800 631
- www.4rs1p.com
- E-mail: info@4roues-sous-1parapluie.com
- Prices: 1¹/₂ hour trip for 3: €54 per person / 3 hour trip for 3: €84 per person
- Romantic evening for two including ride and restaurant: €129 per person

Revisit Paris in a 2CV convertible

"**A** guided tour of the Marais in a "deux-chevaux"? Must be a tourist gimmick!" any blasé Parisian will respond, thinking they already know the city like the back of their hand. But if they can forget their pride for the duration of this highly unusual ride through the streets of the capital, they may change their mind.

Because you never really get to see the whole of Paris. It has accumulated countless – and sometimes undreamt-of – vestiges of the successive stages of its long history. These archaeological clues can be detected at the corner of any street, on building façades, or on the very ground upon which the city stands.

4 Roues sous 1 Parapluie invites you to board one of its fleet of eight 2CVs in order to discover this hidden, unfamiliar or forgotten Paris that conceals a thousand surprising anecdotes. Possessing a solid knowledge of the city's history, our young chauffeur-guide showed us the Revolutionary standard metre at the Ministry of Justice, the head of Joan of Arc indicating the place where she was wounded on rue Saint-Honoré, and the medallions set by artist Jan Dibbets along the Paris meridian running through the Palais-Royal (see Secret Paris in this series of guides). The 2CV then plunges into the streets of the Marais, seeking traces of the neighbourhood's medieval origins. Here, we see a watchtower clinging to a renovated building; over there, we glimpse the signs of past craftsmen. We pass in front of the magnificent Hôtel de Sens and the cannonball embedded in its wall, before pausing to admire the only fig-trees growing in Paris.

Each of the chauffeurs working for the company has their own particular sensibilities, tours are conducted in a very personal manner, and our free-rambling auto ride is nothing like the staid and sometimes boring experience offered by more traditional tours. Although pricey, the ride fulfils its promises, and its richness will satisfy even the most demanding Parisians.

Nevertheless, it's a pity about the almost caricature Montmartre look adopted by the guides – all of them wear traditional caps – no doubt in an attempt to please Japanese or American tourists keen to find that picturesque French touch.

If you are wooing someone special, why not opt for the romantic evening, which includes a 1½ hour ride followed by dinner in a Parisian brasserie? With chauffeur, of course.

ZODIAC RIDES ON THE SEINE,
AND ALONG THE OURCQ AND SAINT-MARTIN CANALS

Contraste association
8 bis, quai d'Amsterdam 93320 Les Pavillons-sous-Bois
• Information and reservations: 01 48 50 37 37 or by e-mail:
contraste@free.fr • http://contraste.free.fr
• Prices: from €55 per person; price quotes based on duration, season
and numbers; group rates for 5 or more

A Zodiac beneath the stars

Do you think the fly-boats on the Seine are too touristy, and their counterparts on Saint-Martin canal too tame? The Contraste association, a team of volunteer enthusiasts, offers à la carte outings on a number of waterways in the Paris region, aboard one of its twenty Zodiac dinghies. The most amusing is no doubt the journey (lasting two good hours) along the Saint-Martin canal from L'Arsenal port at Bastille to La Villette basin.

In addition to an unusual view of the city, the principal interest of this trip is the journey through the superb and mysterious underground section of the canal, almost 2 kilometres long, which stretches between L'Arsenal and rue du Faubourg du Temple. In near-total darkness, except for the light wells that have been hollowed into the pavement on boulevard Richard Lenoir, neon tubes project rainbows on the vault opposite, and you plunge into a fairylike atmosphere that seems completely removed from the heart of Paris.

Once you re-emerge into the open air, negotiating the first lock lets you fully understand the purpose of these immense pools. Numbering nine in all, the locks serve quite simply to allow boats to ascend the 25 metre difference in level separating the Seine from the Ourcq canal.

Immediately after, the crossing beneath the swing bridge at rue Dieu is always a great moment and you're bound to be subject to the curiosity of passers-by (as well as the annoyance of motorists stuck at the red lights on the bank opposite). Those who are still keen can continue their journey all the way to the Sevran forest, gazing up at the stars amidst moorhens and coypus.

Navigating on the Ourcq and Saint-Martin canals being dependent on when the locks close, the last departures are at 21.00 in summer and 19.00 in winter.

DOWN THE CANAL IN AN INFLATABLE

Urban adventurers who dislike travelling in groups can sometimes arrange their own means of covering part of the route described above. Start with a visit to Toys 'R' Us or a similar outlet, and buy the Sévylor or Caravelle 144 inflatable boat that French kids dream about. Don't forget to equip yourself with a foot-pump and an oar. Now take all this gear over to the Saint-Martin canal, at some accessible point between Bastille and Stalingrad. The idea is to simply shove your inflatable boat into the canal, get into it without falling in the water, and then paddle through the more interesting part of the route, the great underground section that leads to Bastille.

NOCTURNAL TOURS OF THE PARIS MÉTRO NETWORK
CONDUCTED BY ADEMAS

- Once a month from September to June (three- to six-month waiting list),
  22.30–5.00 (refreshments offered during the tour, breakfast served at the end)
- 15, rue Erlanger 75016 Paris • Tel: 01 47 46 03 91
- E-mail: ademas@orange.fr • http://ademas.assoc.fr
- Price: €45; members and groups: €40
- Attention: closed temporarily. Reopening soon

**After
the last métro ...**

Following a working week of underground journeys and being jostled by the crowd at Châtelet-Les Halles or Montparnasse stations, it takes a strong sense of cultural curiosity to plunge yet again, on a Saturday at midnight, into the métro. Especially for a tour that lasts around five hours …

Nevertheless, ADEMAS (Association d'Exploitation du Matériel Sprague) regularly gathers together volunteers enthused by the history of the Paris métro and its old Sprague trains. Working for the preservation and restoration of former rolling stock, the association is officially authorized to enter, during the night, the arteries of the underground rail network. Once a month, ADEMAS thus invites the general public to take a seat aboard a train dating from the 1930s for an astonishing trip into the entrails of the city.

These ADEMAS evenings offer a rare opportunity to discover the hidden side of the métro. The tour starts with a visit to the rail workshops owned by the Régie Autonome des Transports Parisiens (RATP – the métro's operating company), located at La Villette. Next you board old rolling stock that runs along the service lines to visit some underground spots now forgotten by everyone: Porte-Molitor and Haxo are two "ghost" stations that were abandoned before they even saw any passengers (see box overleaf). And then there's Croix-Rouge and Saint-Martin, closed to the public since 1939.

As for the Porte-des-Lilas-Cinéma station, it serves today as an experimental and inaugural venue for the RATP. It has also become a studio used to shoot most métro scenes for films and commercials (see *Secret Paris* in this series of guides).

TRENDY HAPPENINGS IN THE MÉTRO
SUBWAY PARTY

- www.aristopunk.com

If the idea of a nocturnal visit to the RATP's underground realm leaves you cold, perhaps you'll be tempted instead by an impromptu party aboard a métro train on the 7 bis line. This trendy annual happening is the brainchild of the event organizers DCONTRACT and Aristopunk. The principle behind this "Subway Party" is to take over the trains using this short shuttle line in north-east Paris and stage a party lasting a few hours …

During the rest of the year, these Party Terrorists occupy other unlikely venues for the space of an evening. To be put in the picture, post a persuasive message on Aristopunk's website.

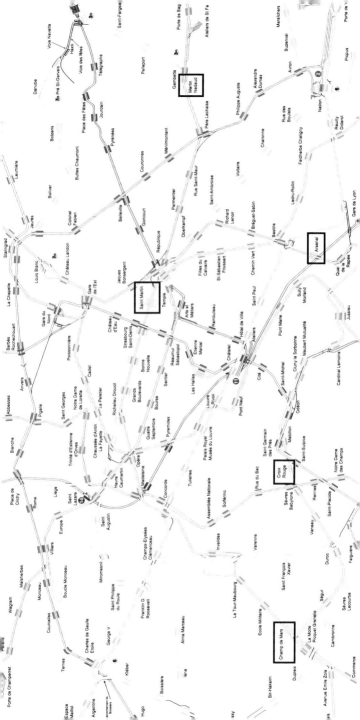

THE PARIS MÉTRO'S GHOST STATIONS

If certain Paris métro stations no longer appear on ordinary maps of the RATP network, they still remain physically present beneath the city's surface and are sometimes used for very different purposes than originally intended …

The closure of most of these so-called "ghost" stations dates from France's entry into the Second World War in 1939: as many of the staff were called up by the army, the métro was forced to operate a reduced network, and following the Liberation those stations that were underused or too close to neighbouring stations were never reopened.

Thus L'Arsenal, Croix-Rouge, Champ-de-Mars, Saint-Martin, Martin-Nadaud and Porte-des-Lilas stations have disappeared from current network maps …

But most of these have in fact found a new calling: in the case of L'Arsenal, classrooms have been installed for training electrical engineers and technicians.

As for Saint-Martin station, whose corridors still bear some beautiful ceramic advertisements on their walls, it sheltered homeless people until its reconversion in 1999 as an "Espace solidarité insertion" run by the French Salvation Army.

The Croix-Rouge station has undergone several changes: at the beginning of the 1980s an artist transformed it into a beach with deck chairs and parasols, and it became the backdrop for various fashion shows.

Lastly, Porte-des-Lilas was converted to use in the cinema industry: behind the platforms still open to the public (part of the station remains connected to the regular network), there are hidden spaces that can be fitted out according to the needs of various film projects, changing names (Pont-Neuf, Pigalle) to suit the director. This part of the station, re-baptized "Porte-des-Lilas-Cinéma", once served a section opened in 1921 that ran to Pré-Saint-Gervais, but was closed in 1939. However, the shuttle on this line still serves to train métro staff and to test new equipment.

Attentive passengers can catch a glimpse from the windows of regular trains of four of these ghost stations: Arsenal, Saint-Martin, Croix-Rouge and Champ-de-Mars.

Haxo station (intended to link Porte-des-Lilas and Pré-Saint-Gervais) and Porte-Molitor (between lines 9 and 10) met with a different fate. Although work on both stations was completed, they were abandoned due to a change in the initial plans, and no outside access was even provided.

CLANDESTINE WALK IN THE CATACOMBS

Access: to be found surfing the Web
• Times: from nightfall until early morning

O ne night in 1897, a group of musicians played requiems by Chopin, Saint-Saëns and Beethoven for an audience of guests invited in secret. The unusual venue for this private concert was 20 metres

*On the trail
of the "cataphiles"*

underground, in a chamber within the catacombs of Paris. As in this anecdote, today the catacombs and their history continue to be a source of inspiration for numerous fringe groups of Parisian society who have staked a claim to the galleries.

Despite the prohibition on entering the catacombs outwith guided tours, it is estimated that there are some 15,000 clandestine visits each year. Well-informed "cataphiles" identify unguarded entries, such as manholes left unsealed by France Telecom technicians, and swap tips on the internet.

Equipped with torches, boots, food and an identity card – in case of an encounter with the police – and above all, reliable maps, the "cataphiles" explore the galleries, some of which lead to magnificent architectural masterpieces, vestiges of quarrying and canal-building within the city.

Although suffering from a rather sinister reputation as a criminal haven right up into the 1980s, when groups of skinheads armed with beer bottles staged pitched battles, the subterranean galleries are also the playground of catacomb fans, heirs to a tradition maintained by student initiates from the Schools of Medicine and Mine Engineering. "Cataphilia", a veritable underground culture in every sense of the term, has its own cult rituals, such as the distribution of whimsical tracts in passageways and locations, such as the "Z chamber", which sometimes welcomes hundreds of participants on special evenings.

LOST IN THE CATACOMBS

Legends and fantasies surround the catacombs and labyrinthine passages. There was, for example, the death of one walker who became lost in the maze, although his disappearance was only reported ... eleven years later, in 1793! He was a porter from the Val-de-Grâce hospital who was attempting to steal liqueurs from Chartreux monastery cellars. He was finally identified thanks to the ring of keys he was carrying. A decorated stele today marks the spot where his body was found.

Beware: unsupervised entry into the catacombs is strictly forbidden. Those who are nevertheless tempted do so at their own risk.

STREET GOLF WITH 19ᴱᴹᴱ TROU

• www.19mtrou.com

Play golf right across Paris

For several years now, a team of five young Parisians, into skating and "streetwear", have been trying to promote their favourite pastime: street golf. The concept is simple, it consists of playing golf anywhere, except on the traditional golf course.

Equipped with recycled clubs and semi-rigid balls, street golfers meet up in Montmartre, on the banks of the Seine, at Stalingrad and Trocadéro … and take out their gear under the surprised but rather amused gaze of passers-by. The object is to devise short rounds and aim at a rubbish bin or an elevated object. Players need a plentiful supply of balls, they tend to go astray after a few minutes.

The idea has recently begun to catch on, and the press has developed an interest in this new fad, leading its erstwhile promoters to hope that it will develop over the next few years. But will this mean a return to grace in France of the preferred sport of the aristocracy and finally allow it to shed its deeply undemocratic image?

It's hard to say today whether young Parisians of 2015 will be going out on Saturday evenings with club and balls to take a few swings with friends. Meanwhile, you can try your hand at the game with the "crew" from 19ème Trou who occasionally organize group sessions. New of upcoming meetings can be found on the collective's website.

HOME THEATRE
WHEN THE THEATRE DROPS INTO YOUR LIVING ROOM ...

You don't need to own a mansion to enjoy the pleasures of putting on a play in your own home: contrary to what you might think, home theatre is neither very expensive, nor very complicated to organize. Most dramatic companies will take care of the whole logistics, opting for short plays that can be staged anywhere and require limited props. Actors all agree on this point: a flat, or even a small studio, can perfectly well becoming the setting for a performance. The price of such services varies from one company to another, but generally run in the range of €20–40 per head of audience.

Although the supply is rich and varied, we have singled out several companies that tend to specialize in this kind of show, as opposed to more classic troupes who only occasionally do shows in private homes.

Performing anything from burlesque to more serious contemporary writing, the companies mentioned favour the conviviality of this form of encounter between the artists and their public, often very warm and much more personal than in a theatre.

Compagnie Peau d'Âmes
• Information and prices: Catherine Chantrel
• Tel: 06 61 73 40 78
• E-mail: peau.d.ames@wanadoo.fr

"If you won't go to the theatre, the theatre will come to you!" That's the philosophy expressed by this company of two actresses, whose project of apartment theatre is rooted in the goal of democratizing contemporary work. A space measuring only 3 by 2 metres will do! Their repertoire offers two plays, both blending humour with gravity.

Benoît Schwartz
• Information and prices: 06 16 98 95 21
• E-mail: Eben.schwartz@wanadoo.fr
• Demo DVD available on request

Alone on stage in your dining room, Benoît Schwartz has developed a particularly original interactive show. The host agrees to prepare a meal in advance according to the recipes given, while the actor deals with the set and lights. The actor himself seats the guests around the table, while secretly attributing a role to each of them. They will thus play a part in his adaptation of *The Princess of Cleves*. But rest assured, they won't be asked to recite a text, just a chance to be an extra!

Pièce montée en aparté
• Information and prices: Charlotte de Fautereau
• Tel: 01 56 08 22 43
• E-mail: chachadefautereau@hotmail.com
• www.piecemontee.net

Bearing out the increasing popularity of home theatre, this association brings together several companies and artists who adapt their shows to the confines of a private flat. They offer musicals, clown acts, stories and plays, for children and adults.

Compagnie Isnt'it
- Information and prices: 01 53 04 99 31
- e-mail: compagnie@isntit.fr
- www.isntit.fr

This company offers four plays encompassing a variety of repertoires: an offbeat adaptation of Little Red Riding Hood, musicals, or more serious pieces. Prices are very modest, for example a rate of €300 for an audience of fifteen to twenty.

In a similar vein to its own humorous shows, the company also runs original theatre classes (annual tuition: €550, one class per week).

design graphique : catherine pöhl · katpoh-mail@yahoo.fr

UNUSUAL HOTEL ROOMS
NO, PARISIAN HOTELS AREN'T JUST FOR TOURISTS
Hospitel – Hôpital Hôtel-Dieu
Galerie B2, 6th floor
1, place du parvis Notre-Dame 75004 Paris
• RER: Saint-Michel; Métro: Cité or Hôtel de Ville
• Tel: 01 44 32 01 00
• www.hotel-hospitel.com • E-mail: hospitelhoteldieu@wanadoo.fr
• Rates: single room: €99; double: €110

Here is the sort of venue you won't come across by accident ... To reach it, you have to enter the precinct of the superb Hôtel Dieu hospital and after crossing the inner courtyard, well worth a visit in its own right, follow the right wing of the building to take the lift up to the 6th floor. A long hallway serves the fourteen garret rooms, half of them offering a – restricted – view of the towers of Notre Dame cathedral.

Arman suite at the Hôtel Lutetia
45, boulevard Raspail 75006 Paris
• Métro: Sèvres Babylone
• Tel: 01 49 54 46 46
• www.lutetia-paris.com • E-mail: lutetia-paris@lutetia-paris.com
• Rates: €3,000

In 1995 the Hôtel Lutetia, icon of the Left Bank, inaugurated a suite (two bedrooms, two bathrooms, lounge and balcony), conceived and decorated by the French-born American artist Arman. Throughout the 135 m^2 of the luxurious apartment, the artist has developed the theme of music and stringed instruments: the sofa and two chairs in the lounge as well as the maple headboard of the bed are cello-shaped. Other sculptures by Arman share space with collector's items chosen by the artist. Unique.

Concept room at the Hôtel Sofitel Arc de Triomphe
14, rue Beaujon 75008 Paris
• Métro: Charles de Gaulle
• Tel: 01 53 89 50 50 • E-mail: H1296@accor.com
• Rates: on request from hotel reservations

Putting into practice the results of studies by the Research and Style department of the Accor hotel chain on the likely components of tomorrow's hotel room, a "concept room" was born in room 217 of the Sofitel Arc de Triomphe. Futuristic equipment is tested here in vivo: the visual setting can be modulated using individually adjustable light sources, perfumed micromolecules can be dispersed in each room, offering a choice of six olfactory ambiences in the bedroom and two in the bathroom. A plasma screen lets you watch television or surf the internet from anywhere in the room, thanks to an articulated arm that pivots through 120°. All this, of course, can be remotely controlled from a tactile screen accessible from the bed.

Bateau Pytheas Vivas
Port des Champs-Élysées 75008 Paris
• http://perso.orange.fr/chambredhote.paris/fr/accueil.html
• Rates: €150 per night, including breakfast
(10% reduction from 4th night)

Quirkily installed on a river barge moored between the Assemblée Nationale and place de la Concorde, this unusual and romantic guest room is perfect for Parisian couples looking for a change of scenery.

"Fresco room" at the Hôtel des Saints-Pères
65, rue des Saints-Pères 75006 Paris
• Métro: Saint-Germain-des-Près or Saint-Sulpice
• Tel: 01 45 44 50 00
• www.esprit-de-France.com • E-mail: hsp@espritfrance.com
• Rates: €345

Only a few shrewd Parisians know about the "fresco room" at the Hôtel des Saints-Pères. This was originally part of a private townhouse belonging to an architect in the service of Louis XIV, Daniel Gittard, who made it his residence in the 17th century. The room is decorated with a magnificent ceiling which has been meticulously preserved and subtly enhanced by adapted lighting, embellished by a fresco painted by students of the Versailles School. Perfect for a romantic escapade.

Hôtel des Saints-Pères © Arnaud Frich

MUSEUMS OPEN IN THE EVENING

Musée du Louvre
- Métro: Palais Royal-Musée du Louvre
- Open daily 9.00–18.00, except Tuesday
- Wednesday and Friday evenings until 22.00
- Admission: €8.50 / €6 (evening)

Musée des Arts et Métiers
60, rue Réaumur 75003 Paris
- Métro: Arts et Métiers or Réaumur-Sébastopol
- www.arts-et-metiers.net
- Open Tuesday to Sunday, 10.00–18.00
- Thursday evening until 21.30
- Closed Monday and public holidays
- Lectures held on certain Thursdays at 18.30
- Admission: €6.50 / €4.50

Musée d'Orsay
62, rue de Lille 75007 Paris
- Métro: Solférino; RER: Musée d'Orsay
- www.musee-orsay.fr
- Open Tuesday to Sunday, 9.30–18.00
- Thursday evening until 21.45
- Closed on Monday
- Admission: €7.50 / €5.50 (from 20.00 on Thursday)

Cité de l'Architecture et du Patrimoine
Temporary exhibition galleries
45, avenue du Président Wilson 75116 Paris
Galeries d'actualité/ Auditorium/ Salon de l'IFA/ École de Chaillot
7, avenue Albert de Mun 75116 Paris
- Métro: Trocadéro or Iéna; RER: Champ de Mars-Tour Eiffel
- www.citechaillot.fr
- Open weekdays, except Tuesday, 12.00–20.00; Saturday and Sunday, 11.00–19.00
- Thursday evening until 22.00
- Admission: free for temporary galleries and exhibitions: €5 / €3

Musée de L'Érotisme
72, boulevard de Clichy 75018 Paris
- Métro: Blanche
- Tel: 01 42 58 28 73
- www.musee-erotisme.com
- Open daily 10.00–2.00
- Admission: €8 / €6

Open until 2 in the morning and naturally enough located among the sex shops of Pigalle, the Musée de l'Érotisme offers seven floors of an interesting and, above all, cultural and historical perspective on both ancient and modern erotic art from the five continents. Including Greek vases, Aztec figurines, Japanese prints, and photos from the early 20th century, the modes of expression vary but all attempt to portray the importance of sex within society. One must-see exhibit: "Las auténticas peliculas X de época", a Spanish collection of pornographic movies from the 1920s, filmed at the request of King Alfonso XIII.

EVENING SWIMMING
Club Quartier Latin
19, rue de Pontoise 75005 Paris • Métro: Maubert-Mutualité
• Tel: 01 55 42 77 88 • www.clubquartierlatin.com
• Open Monday to Wenesday and Friday, 20.15-23.45; Thursday,
21.00-23.45 • Same hours during school holidays (except Thursday,
open 20.15–23.45)
• Admission: €9.50

Better known as the "Piscine Pontoise", this pool is a meeting-place for dynamic executives, insomniac athletes and Parisian gays. Once night has fallen, only the projectors at the bottom of the pool provide illumination, plunging the immense hall into a rather aesthetic semi-darkness.

Piscine Joséphine Baker
Quai de la Gare 75013 Paris • Métro: Quai de la Gare or Bercy
• Tel: 01 56 61 96 50 • Open until midnight Tuesday; until 21.00 Monday,
Wednesday; until 23.00 Thursday; until 22.00 Friday, and until 20.00 Saturday,
Sunday and public holidays • Admission: €2.60; concessions: €1.50

This new swimming pool 90 metres in length, open-air in summer, floats
on the Seine ... A solarium and fitness centre await you when you emerge
from the pool.

Blue fitness Eiffel
Hôtel Novotel Paris Tour Eiffel: 61, quai de Grenelle 75015 Paris
• RER/Métro: Javel; Métro: Bir-Hakeim or Charles-Michel
• Tel: 01 45 75 25 45 • Open Monday to Friday 8.00–22.00; Saturday
8.00–21.00; Sunday and public holidays 10.00–18.00
• Admission: €14 (pool + sauna); concessions for hotel guests

From the small but elegant pool and the cardio machines of the Blue fitness
centre, the view takes in the Seine embankments and the Radio France building. Ideal for the young and upwardly mobile. It's said that French supermo-
del Laetitia Casta comes by regularly.

Espace sportif Pailleron
32, rue Édouard Pailleron 75019 Paris • Métro: Bolivar • Tel: 01 40 40 27 70
• Open Monday to Thursday until 22.30, Friday to Saturday until midnight,
and Sunday until 18.00 • Admission: €3.10 / €4.80 after 20.00; concessions:
€1.80 / €2.70 after 20.00

The new Espace Pailleron is an attractive addition to the city's municipal
pools: recently renovated, this one has preserved, as a feast for the eye,
the original two tiers of changing cabins. The centre also houses the sole
municipal skating rink in Paris, open until midnight on Saturday, a fitness
and bodybuilding room, sauna and restaurant.

Subaqua Club de Paris
• Every Friday, 20.30–22.30 (enquire with the association to access the
pool being used) • www.subaquaparis.org • E-mail: info@subaquaparis.org
• First trial: free • Club membership + training: €280

This group of underwater diving enthusiasts trains every week ... in a swimming pool! For newcomers, the Subaqua Club of Paris offers a free trial dive
using an air bottle: it's a chance to experience the magic sensations of underwater diving, before attempting a more comprehensive training course.

Centre Aquatique municipal de Neuilly-sur-Seine
27–31, boulevard d'Inkermann 92200 Neuilly-sur-Seine
• Métro: Sablons • Pay parking only
• Tel: 01 41 92 02 20 • Open Tuesday and Friday evenings, 16.30–23.00
• Admission: €5.10 / €4.60 after 19.00; concessions: €4.10 / €3.70 after 19.00

The gardens surrounding the building and the giant screen displaying the latest
news of the pool plunge you into an affluent ambience before you even enter
the premises. The complex includes a large pool, a covered play-pool that extends into the open air, a waterslide, a wading pool, and even a solarium.

Piscine de Nogent-sur-Marne
8, rue du Port, Nogent-sur-Marne • RER: A or E lines
• Tel: 01 48 71 37 92 • Open Wednesday and Friday evenings until 22.00
• Admission: €6.90

PARISIAN UFOLOGY DINNERS

Casino cafeteria, Les Quatre Temps shopping centre (Place de la Défense)
92000 La Défense
- RER/Métro: La Défense
- First Tuesday of the month, from 19.00 to around 22.30
- Information: Gérard Labat at 01 69 31 04 90 or 06 74 86 15 46
- E-mail: labat@aol.com
- http://www.les-repas-ufologiques.com
- Admission free, meals payable to cafeteria

Close encounters of the third kind at La Défense

Until now you've been living in ignorance as just another victim of institutional lies. But buy yourself steak and chips at the Quatre Temps Casino cafeteria, go on up to the restaurant's first floor, and there you'll enjoy the privilege of learning the whole truth about UFOs.

On the first Tuesday of every month, this self-service restaurant plays host to around a hundred fans of ufology, the study of unidentified flying objects and other strange phenomena associated with extraterrestrial contact.

The regulars at these encounters of the third kind look just like other conventional human being. The proliferation of moustaches and checked shirts, however, distinguishes them from the middle-management types walking down the esplanade of La Défense as offices close. If you look a little closer, you'll notice that the average ufologist tends to be a man in his fifties at least.

As they rarely have anywhere suitable to display their work in public, ufologists take advantage of these gatherings to announce the publication of books, articles, magazines or reports on flying saucers. Before the lecture scheduled for 20.30, they trade books dealing with the paranormal: "Hey, I just finished Strange Creatures from Outer Space, it's got a really interesting angle on the subject …"

The existence of extraterrestrial intelligence and the imminence of first contact with our planet seems to be a conviction widely shared among all those present. But, as we know only too well, "They're hiding the truth about UFOs from us!" with both the French government and the Parisian media colluding in the cover-up … Will there be contact with us Earthlings? One thing is for sure by the end of the evening: these ufologists certainly don't harbour any hostile intentions towards the rest of us, so you can join them without fear.

LA FERME DU BONHEUR

220, avenue de la République 92000 Nanterre
- SNCF/RER: Nanterre-Université
- Tel: 01 47 24 51 24
- E-mail: la.ferme.du.bonheur@free.fr

An alternative farm on the outskirts of Paris

When you take the access ramp leading to the university campus from the SNCF/RER railway station at Nanterre, it's difficult to imagine that a "farm" could have grown up and survived in such an inhospitable environment. Yet it is between the drab modern university buildings and the A86 motorway that the Ferme du Bonheur has elected to set up residence.

To reach the farm from the station, you need to walk across the campus, past the tennis courts towards the big tops of the neighbouring circus school.

Founded nearly almost fifteen years ago by Roger des Prés, who calls himself a "show farmer", the farm is perhaps more deserving of its "alternative" label than anywhere else in the Paris region. Its very existence on waste ground defies all urban logic. Just step inside the gate to find yourself in another world, light years from the harsh architecture of Nanterre, omnipresent though that is. The imposing old wooden gate, topped by a bell, announces the whole tone of this enchanting, surreally ironic establishment, unlike any other we've visited. In a small garden nearby, a grand piano is quietly rotting away.

Beyond its agricultural activities (chickens, goats, rabbits and various crops are raised here), the farm organizes occasional cultural events: poetry readings, harpsichord concerts, plays and exhibitions are all hosted here beneath a vast tent cluttered with disparate objects.

The place therefore combines features of a farm, a gypsy camp (the offices are in caravans), and a rustic restaurant. The large dance hall, now undergoing building work to bring it up to standard, will soon reopen for evening entertainment. We strongly recommend that you e-mail to sign up for their newsletter and keep up to date with events.

JUGGLING EVENINGS AT L'ÉCOLE ÉPITA

24, rue Pasteur 94276 Kremlin-Bicêtre
- Métro: Porte-d'Italie or Le Kremlin-Bicêtre
- Every Monday from 20.00 to midnight
- Annual subscription €15

Diabolo in an underground car park

Stuck in a nondescript residential neighbourhood in the suburb of Kremlin-Bicêtre, just a short distance from the boulevard Périphérique, the Épita information technology college has an unlikely underground car park now put to other uses by student organizations.

The C Comme Cirque association, formed by the students, hosts meetings by jugglers from all over Paris on Monday evenings, in exchange for an annual fee of €15 per head.

Once you descend the access ramp, you enter a setting worthy of a television studio: an immense neon-lit space whose walls are entirely covered with graffiti. A merry mess of junk lies in every corner and freight containers have been converted into offices for the associations. With its high ceilings, this space is ideal for practising juggling with diabolo, skittles or balls.

The atmosphere is of course very cool, and casual good nature abounds.

Although these meetings are primarily reserved for jugglers, feel free to simply come along and watch.

TOUR OF THE MARCHÉ INTERNATIONAL DE RUNGIS

Coach departs place Denfert-Rochereau for Rungis
- Second Friday of the month
- Departure time 5.00 if there is a minimum of 20 bookings
- Reservations: resa@visiterungis.com
- www.visiterungis.com
- Price: €65 including breakfast with a charcuterie, cheeses, desserts and drinks (mineral water, wine, coffee)

Leave at 5 for an unusual "morning after" party ...

Although a visit to the international market at Rungis might not be a clubbers' dream, it does represent an ideal "morning after" party for those seeking a truly extraordinary way to end the evening ... But the experience is also worthwhile to any early risers ...

The experience starts on the second Friday of the month at place Denfert-Rochereau. The time is exactly 5 in the morning, Paris is waking and so are you, unless, thanks to your superhuman endurance or consumption of illicit substances, you still haven't gone to bed ...

Half an hour later, the coach drops you at the world's largest fresh produce market, spread out over vast space of 232 hectares.

The tour offers a unique opportunity for private individuals, not in possession of a wholesaler's card, to immerse themselves in this giant food fair, organized around five main pavilions: seafood, meat, dairy produce ("the biggest cheeseboard in the world", as you might expect in France), fruit and vegetables, and cut flowers.

There is nothing more picturesque than to stroll through this market observing the rhythm of the deliveries and the hard bargaining that takes place thereafter, and to soak up the once characteristic atmosphere of the Paris street scene was lost to the city centre when the market decamped from Les Halles towards the outskirts.

By around 6, you'll have amply earned your "Rungis breakfast". Be warned that this is rather more copious than the usual coffee and croissant ...

© Marché International de Rungis

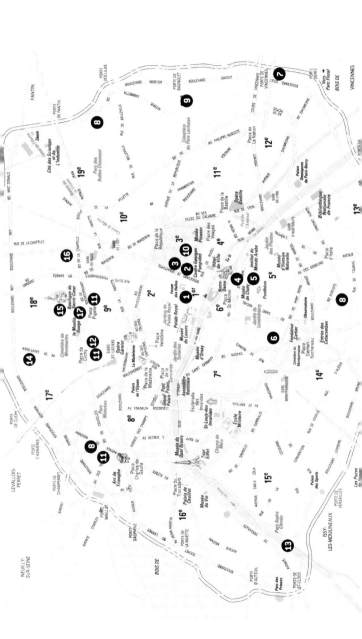

VERSIFYING VAULT ❶
La cave à poèmes
3, rue des Déchargeurs 75001 Paris — See page 22

COMMUNE TO THE SOUND OF DIDGERIDOOS ❷
Group didgeridoo classes with the Vent du Rêve association
Imprévu Café
9, rue Quincampoix 75004 Paris — See page 32

IMAGINE WHAT IT'S LIKE TO BE BLIND ... ❸
DINE IN PITCH BLACKNESS
Dans le Noir
51, rue Quincampoix 75004 Paris — See page 34

TAKE A NAP IN A BOOKSHOP ❹
The bed at Shakespeare & Company, the English-language bookshop
37, rue de la Bûcherie 75005 Paris — See page 38

SKYWATCHING AT THE SORBONNE ❺
Observatoire de la Société astronomique de France
Université de la Sorbonne — See page 42

LITTLE-KNOWN READINGS AT REID HALL ❻
"Textes & Voix": evening readings
See page 48

SKINNY-DIPPING ❼
Nude swimming at Centre nautique Roger Le Gall
34, boulevard Carnot 75012 Paris — See page 72

A CURIOUS BELGIAN FAITH ... ❽
Temple Antoiniste
See page 78

ALTERNATIVE PUPPETRY AND EXPERIMENTAL MUSIC ❾
Théâtre l'Ogresse
4, rue des Prairies — corner of 125, rue de Bagnolet 75020 Paris — See page 106

DIABOLO
IN AN UNDERGROUND CAR PARK
Juggling evenings at L'École Épita
24, rue Pasteur 94276 Kremlin-Bicêtre — See page 140

MONDAY, BUT ALSO EVERY EVENING

THERE WAS A GUY TAKING A SHOWER ... **⑩**
Raidd Bar – 23, rue du Temple 75003 Paris – See page 28

LE MULTICOLORE: PARISIAN ROULETTE **⑪**
See page 114

THE COLOUR OF MONEY **⑫**
Cercle Clichy-Montmartre: 84, rue de Clichy 75009 Paris – See page 56

A PHONE BOX UNLIKE ANY OTHER ... **⑬**
Sophie Calle's phone box
Pont du Garigliano 75015 Paris – See page 82

"HOUZE" OF HAPPINESS **⑭**
La Maizon – 13, rue Collette 75017 Paris – See page 92

NUIT D'ADORATION AU SACRÉ-CŒUR **⑮**
35, rue du Chevalier-de-la-Barre 75018 Paris – See page 94

BREAKING THE ICE AT 5 BELOW ZERO **⑯**
Ice Bar de l'hôtel Kube – 1-5, passage Ruelle 75018 Paris – See page 100

MUSÉE DE L'ÉROTISME **⑰**
72, boulevard de Clichy 75018 Paris – See page 133

CRASHING CELEBRITY PARTIES WITH THE SYNDICAT DU HYPE
See page 109

ENJOY YOUR FIFTEEN MINUTES OF FAME
Soirée de star – See page 110

REVISIT PARIS IN A 2CV CONVERTIBLE
"Deux-chevaux" rides around Paris with 4 Roues sous 1 Parapluie – See page 116

A ZODIAC BENEATH THE STARS
Zodiac rides on the Seine, and along the Ourcq and Saint-Martin canals – Voir page 118

ON THE TRAIL OF THE "CATAPHILES"
Clandestine walk in the catacombs – See page 124

PLAY GOLF RIGHT ACROSS PARIS
Streetgolf with 19ème Trou – See page 126

INVITE A PSYCHIC INTO YOUR LIVING ROOM
Paranormal demonstrations with Erick Fearson
See page 71

EVENING SWIMMING
Pools – See page 134

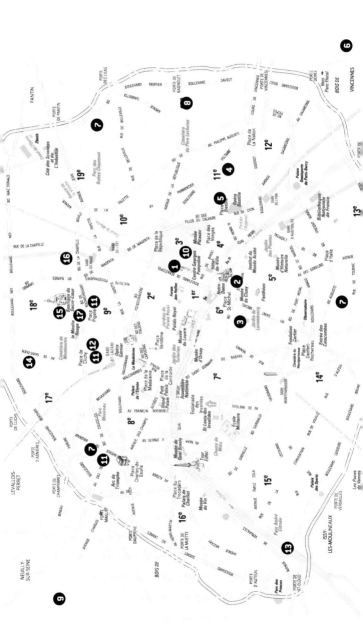

IMAGINE WHAT IT'S LIKE TO BE BLIND ... ❶
DINE IN PITCH BLACKNESS
Dans le Noir

51, rue Quincampoix 75004 Paris – See page 34

TAKE A NAP IN A BOOKSHOP ❷
The bed at Shakespeare & Company, the English-language bookshop

37, rue de la Bûcherie 75005 Paris
See page 38

A NIGHT AT THE SENATE ❸
Late-night sittings

Visitors' entrance at 15, rue de Vaugirard 75006 Paris
See page 46

HEALING LAUGHTER ❹
Yoga du rire

6 bis, rue Jean-Macé 75011 Paris
See page 64

TAROT READINGS ❺
Le Bar sans Nom

49, rue de Lappe 75011 Paris
See page 68

PLUNGE INTO THE UNIVERSE OF RACEGOERS ❻
Evening races at the Hippodrome de Vincennes

2, route de la Ferme 75012 Paris (bois de Vincennes)
See page 74

A CURIOUS BELGIAN FAITH ... ❼
Temple antoiniste

See page 78

ALTERNATIVE PUPPETRY AND EXPERIMENTAL MUSIC ❽
Théâtre l'Ogresse

4, rue des Prairies – angle 125, rue de Bagnolet 75020 Paris
See page 106

CLOSE ENCOUNTERS OF THE THIRD KIND AT LA DÉFENSE ❾
Parisian ufology dinners

Cafétéria Casino, centre commercial Les Quatre Temps (Place de la Défense)
See page 136

TUESDAY, BUT ALSO EVERY EVENING

THERE WAS A GUY TAKING A SHOWER … !   **⑩**
Raidd Bar – 23, rue du Temple 75003 Paris – See page 28

LE MULTICOLORE: LA ROULETTE PARISIENNE   **⑪**
See page 114

THE COLOUR OF MONEY   **⑫**
Cercle Clichy-Montmartre. 84, rue de Clichy 75009 Paris – See page 56

A PHONE BOX UNLIKE ANY OTHER...   **⑬**
Sophie Calle's phone box
Pont du Garigliano 75015 Paris – See page 82

"HOUZE" OF HAPPINESS   **⑭**
La Maizon – 13, rue Collette 75017 Paris – See page 92

NIGHT OF ADORATION AT SACRÉ-CŒUR   **⑮**
35, rue du Chevalier-de-la-Barre 75018 Paris – See page 94

BREAKING THE ICE AT 5 BELOW ZERO   **⑯**
Ice Bar de l'hôtel Kube – 1-5, passage Ruelle 75018 Paris – See page 100

MUSÉE DE L'ÉROTISME   **⑰**
72, boulevard de Clichy 75018 Paris – See page 133

CRASHING CELEBRITY PARTIES WITH THE SYNDICAT DU HYPE
See page 109

ENJOY YOUR FIFTEEN MINUTES OF FAME
Soirée de star – See page 110

REVISIT PARIS IN A 2CV CONVERTIBLE
"Deux-chevaux" rides around Paris with 4 Roues sous 1 Parapluie – See page 116

A ZODIAC BENEATH THE STARS
Zodiac rides on the Seine, and along the Ourcq and Saint-Martin canals – Voir page 118

ON THE TRAIL OF THE "CATAPHILES"
Clandestine walk in the catacombs – See page 124

PLAY GOLF RIGHT ACROSS PARIS
Streetgolf with 19ème Trou – See page 126

INVITE A PSYCHIC INTO YOUR LIVING ROOM
Paranormal demonstrations with Erick Fearson
See page 71

EVENING SWIMMING
Pools – See page 134

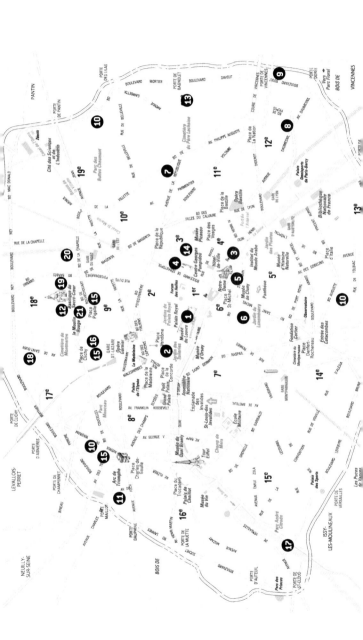

MUSÉE DU LOUVRE ❶
See page 133

CHIC SUÈDE ❷
Cercle suédois — 242, rue de Rivoli 75001 Paris — See page 12

PREPARE FOR A FREIGHTER TRIP ❸
Cargo Club apéro at Librairie Ulysse

26, rue Saint Louis en l'Ile 75004 Paris — See page 30

IMAGINE WHAT IT'S LIKE TO BE BLIND ... ❹
DINE IN PITCH BLACKNESS
Dans le Noir

51, rue Quincampoix 75004 Paris — See page 34

TAKE A NAP IN A BOOKSHOP ❺
The bed at Shakespeare & Company, the English-language bookshop

37, rue de la Bûcherie 75005 Paris — See page 38

A NIGHT AT THE SENATE ❻
Late-night sittings

Visitors' entrance at 15, rue de Vaugirard 75006 Paris — See page 46

"IT'S PERMANENT, SURE, BUT ON SOMETHING THAT'S ONLY TEMPORARY ..." ❼
L'homme tatoué — 13, rue Moret 75011 Paris — See page 60

TAROT READINGS WITH ALEXANDRO JODOROWSKY ❽
Le Téméraire — 32, avenue Dausmenil 75012 Paris — See page 68

SKINNY-DIPPING ❾
Nude swimming at Centre nautique Roger Le Gall

Centre nautique Roger Le Gall : 34, boulevard Carnot 75012 Paris — See page 72

A CURIOUS BELGIAN FAITH ... ❿
Temple antoiniste — See page 78

DISCOVER THE BAHÁ'Í FAITH ⓫
Bahá'í Wednesday talks

Centre bahá'í — 45, rue Pergolèse 75116 Paris — See page 86

A LOVE SEAT FOR TWO ⓬
Ciné 13 Théâtre — 1, avenue Junot 75018 Paris — See page 96

ALTERNATIVE PUPPETRY AND EXPERIMENTAL MUSIC ⓭
Théâtre l'Ogresse — 4, rue des Prairies 75020 Paris — See page 106

WEDNESDAY, BUT ALSO EVERY EVENING

THERE WAS A GUY TAKING A SHOWER ... ! ⓮
Raidd Bar – 23, rue du Temple 75003 Paris – See page 28

LE MULTICOLORE: LA ROULETTE PARISIENNE ⓯
See page 114

THE COLOUR OF MONEY ⓰
Cercle Clichy-Montmartre. 84, rue de Clichy 75009 Paris – See page 56

A PHONE BOX UNLIKE ANY OTHER... ⓱
Sophie Calle's phone box
Pont du Garigliano 75015 Paris – See page 82

"HOUZE" OF HAPPINESS ⓲
La Maizon – 13, rue Collette 75017 Paris – See page 92

NIGHT OF ADORATION AT SACRÉ-CŒUR ⓳
35, rue du Chevalier-de-la-Barre 75018 Paris – See page 94

BREAKING THE ICE AT 5 BELOW ZERO ⓴
Ice Bar de l'hôtel Kube – 1-5, passage Ruelle 75018 Paris – See page 100

MUSÉE DE L'ÉROTISME ㉑
72, boulevard de Clichy 75018 Paris – See page 133

CRASHING CELEBRITY PARTIES WITH THE SYNDICAT DU HYPE
See page 109

ENJOY YOUR FIFTEEN MINUTES OF FAME
Soirée de star – See page 110

REVISIT PARIS IN A 2CV CONVERTIBLE
"Deux-chevaux" rides around Paris with 4 Roues sous 1 Parapluie – See page 116

A ZODIAC BENEATH THE STARS
Zodiac rides on the Seine, and along the Ourcq and Saint-Martin canals – Voir page 118

ON THE TRAIL OF THE "CATAPHILES"
Clandestine walk in the catacombs – See page 124

PLAY GOLF RIGHT ACROSS PARIS
Streetgolf with 19ᵉᵐᵉ Trou – See page 126

INVITE A PSYCHIC INTO YOUR LIVING ROOM
Paranormal demonstrations with Erick Fearson
See page 71

EVENING SWIMMING
Pools – See page 134

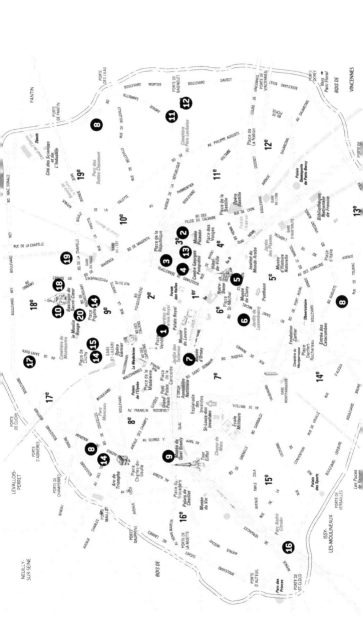

CHOOSE A SEX TOY OVER A GLASS OF CHAMPAGNE ❶
« Apéro coquin»

11, rue du Marché Saint Honoré 75001 Paris — See page 14

EVENING READINGS FROM ANOTHER CENTURY ❷
Bibliothèque des Amis de l'Instruction of the 3rd *arrondissement*

54, rue de Turenne 75003 Paris — See page 26

MUSÉE DES ARTS ET MÉTIERS ❸

60, rue Réaumur 75003 Paris — See page 133

IMAGINE WHAT IT'S LIKE TO BE BLIND … ❹
DINE IN PITCH BLACKNESS
Dans le Noir

51, rue Quincampoix 75004 Paris — See page 34

TAKE A NAP IN A BOOKSHOP ❺
The bed at Shakespeare & Company, the English-language bookshop

37, rue de la Bûcherie 75005 Paris — See page 38

A NIGHT AT THE SENATE ❻
Late-night sittings

Visitors' entrance at 15, rue de Vaugirard 75006 Paris — See page 46

MUSÉE D'ORSAY ❼

62, rue de Lille 75007 Paris — See page 133

A CURIOUS BELGIAN FAITH … ❽
Temple antoiniste — See page 78

CITÉ DE L'ARCHITECTURE ET DU PATRIMOINE ❾

See page 135

A LOVE SEAT FOR TWO ❿
Ciné 13 Théâtre

1, avenue Junot 75018 Paris — See page 96

A MUSIC LESSON AT THE TOWN HALL ⓫
Music lessons from Jean-François Zygel

Mairie du XXe arrondissement — 6, place Gambetta 75020 Paris — See page 104

ALTERNATIVE PUPPETRY AND EXPERIMENTAL MUSIC ⓬
Théâtre l'Ogresse

4, rue des Prairies — angle 125, rue de Bagnolet 75020 Paris — See page 106

THURSDAY, BUT ALSO EVERY EVENING

THERE WAS A GUY TAKING A SHOWER … ! **⓭**
Raidd Bar – 23, rue du Temple 75003 Paris – See page 28

LE MULTICOLORE: LA ROULETTE PARISIENNE **⓮**
See page 114

THE COLOUR OF MONEY **⓯**
Cercle Clichy-Montmartre. 84, rue de Clichy 75009 Paris – See page 56

A PHONE BOX UNLIKE ANY OTHER… **⓰**
Sophie Calle's phone box
Pont du Garigliano 75015 Paris – See page 82

"HOUZE" OF HAPPINESS **⓱**
La Maizon – 13, rue Collette 75017 Paris – See page 92

NIGHT OF ADORATION AT SACRÉ-CŒUR **⓲**
35, rue du Chevalier-de-la-Barre 75018 Paris – See page 94

BREAKING THE ICE AT 5 BELOW ZERO **⓳**
Ice Bar de l'hôtel Kube – 1-5, passage Ruelle 75018 Paris – See page 100

MUSÉE DE L'ÉROTISME **⓴**
72, boulevard de Clichy 75018 Paris – See page 133

CRASHING CELEBRITY PARTIES WITH THE SYNDICAT DU HYPE
See page 109

ENJOY YOUR FIFTEEN MINUTES OF FAME
Soirée de star – See page 110

REVISIT PARIS IN A 2CV CONVERTIBLE
"Deux-chevaux" rides around Paris with 4 Roues sous 1 Parapluie – See page 116

A ZODIAC BENEATH THE STARS
Zodiac rides on the Seine, and along the Ourcq and Saint-Martin canals – Voir page 118

ON THE TRAIL OF THE "CATAPHILES"
Clandestine walk in the catacombs – See page 124

PLAY GOLF RIGHT ACROSS PARIS
Streetgolf with 19ème Trou – See page 126

INVITE A PSYCHIC INTO YOUR LIVING ROOM
Paranormal demonstrations with Erick Fearson
See page 71

EVENING SWIMMING
Pools – See page 134

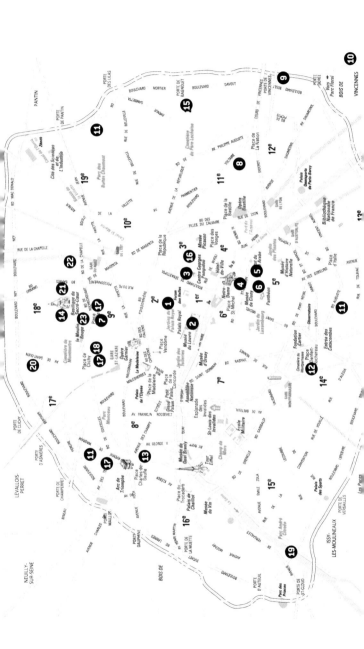

LIVE FROM THE OTHER SIDE
Clairvoyant experience at USFIPES

15 rue Jean-Jacques Rousseau 75001 Paris
See page 18

MUSÉE DU LOUVRE

See page 133

IMAGINE WHAT IT'S LIKE TO BE BLIND ...
DINE IN PITCH BLACKNESS
Dans le Noir

51, rue Quincampoix 75004 Paris
See page 34

TAKE A NAP IN A BOOKSHOP
The bed at Shakespeare & Company, the English-language bookshop

37, rue de la Bûcherie 75005 Paris
See page 38

A RE-ANIMATED CROWD
The Rocky Horror Picture Show

Cinéma Studio Galande
42, rue Galande 75005 Paris
See page 40

SKYWATCHING AT THE SORBONNE
Observatoire de la Société astronomique de France

Université de la Sorbonne
See page 42

MUST BE SEEN TO BE BELIEVED
Escualita: transsexual evenings at the Folies Pigalle

Folie's Pigalle
11, place Pigalle 75009 Paris
See page 58

BRING YOUR OWN CHAIR TO A FILM CLUB
Le Ciné-club des Artisans

5, cité de l'Ameublement 75011 Paris
See page 66

SKINNY-DIPPING
Nude swimming at Centre nautique Roger Le Gall

Centre nautique Roger Le Gall
34, boulevard Carnot 75012 Paris
See page 72

PLUNGE INTO THE UNIVERSE OF RACEGOERS 🔟
Evening races at the Hippodrome de Vincennes

2, route de la Ferme 75012 Paris (bois de Vincennes)
See page 74

A CURIOUS BELGIAN FAITH ... ⑪
Temple antoiniste
See page 78

CONCERTS IN A "BABA COOL" CABIN ⑫
Le 24 bis

24 bis, rue Gassendi 75014 Paris
See page 81

DELVING INTO THE SECRETS OF THE GREAT ARCHITECT ⑬
Loge unie des théosophes

11 bis, rue Kepler 75116 Paris
See page 84

A LOVE SEAT FOR TWO ⑭
Ciné 13 Théâtre

1, avenue Junot 75018 Paris
See page 96

ALTERNATIVE PUPPETRY AND EXPERIMENTAL MUSIC ⑮
Théâtre l'Ogresse

4, rue des Prairies – angle 125, rue de Bagnolet 75020 Paris
See page 106

Déesse Clito

FRIDAY, BUT ALSO EVERY EVENING

THERE WAS A GUY TAKING A SHOWER ... !　**❶⑥**
Raidd Bar – 23, rue du Temple 75003 Paris – See page 28

LE MULTICOLORE: LA ROULETTE PARISIENNE　**❶⑦**
See page 114

THE COLOUR OF MONEY　**❶⑧**
Cercle Clichy-Montmartre. 84, rue de Clichy 75009 Paris – See page 56

A PHONE BOX UNLIKE ANY OTHER...　**❶⑨**
Sophie Calle's phone box
Pont du Garigliano 75015 Paris – See page 82

"HOUZE" OF HAPPINESS　**❷⓪**
La Maizon – 13, rue Collette 75017 Paris – See page 92

NIGHT OF ADORATION AT SACRÉ-CŒUR　**❷①**
35, rue du Chevalier-de-la-Barre 75018 Paris – See page 94

BREAKING THE ICE AT 5 BELOW ZERO　**❷②**
Ice Bar de l'hôtel Kube – 1-5, passage Ruelle 75018 Paris – See page 100

MUSÉE DE L'ÉROTISME　**❷③**
72, boulevard de Clichy 75018 Paris – See page 133

CRASHING CELEBRITY PARTIES WITH THE SYNDICAT DU HYPE
See page 109

ENJOY YOUR FIFTEEN MINUTES OF FAME
Soirée de star – See page 110

REVISIT PARIS IN A 2CV CONVERTIBLE
"Deux-chevaux" rides around Paris with 4 Roues sous 1 Parapluie – See page 116

A ZODIAC BENEATH THE STARS
Zodiac rides on the Seine, and along the Ourcq and Saint-Martin canals – Voir page 118

ON THE TRAIL OF THE "CATAPHILES"
Clandestine walk in the catacombs – See page 124

PLAY GOLF RIGHT ACROSS PARIS
Streetgolf with 19ème Trou – See page 126

INVITE A PSYCHIC INTO YOUR LIVING ROOM
Paranormal demonstrations with Erick Fearson
See page 71

EVENING SWIMMING
Pools – See page 134

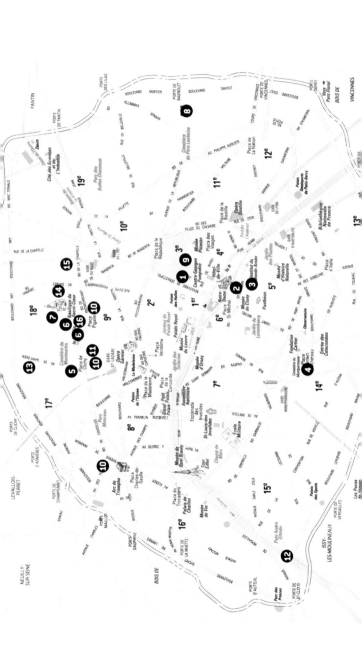

IMAGINE WHAT IT'S LIKE TO BE BLIND … ❶
DINE IN PITCH BLACKNESS
Dans le Noir

51, rue Quincampoix 75004 Paris – See page 34

TAKE A NAP IN A BOOKSHOP ❷
The bed at Shakespeare & Company, the English-language bookshop

37, rue de la Bûcherie 75005 Paris
See page 38

A RE-ANIMATED CROWD ❸
The Rocky Horror Picture Show

Cinéma Studio Galande
42, rue Galande 75005 Paris
See page 40

CONCERTS IN A "BABA COOL" CABIN ❹
Le 24 bis

24 bis, rue Gassendi 75014 Paris
See page 81

THE BIGGEST FETISHIST EVENING IN PARIS ❺
La Nuit Élastique

Caves Lechapelais
7, rue Lechapelais 75017 Paris
See page 90

DINNER IN A MODERN ART LOFT-GALLERY ❻
The Box in Paris

6, cité du Midi, 75018 Paris
See page 99

A LOVE SEAT FOR TWO ❼
Ciné 13 Théâtre

1, avenue Junot 75018 Paris
See page 96

ALTERNATIVE PUPPETRY AND EXPERIMENTAL MUSIC ❽
Théâtre l'Ogresse

4, rue des Prairies – angle 125, rue de Bagnolet 75020 Paris
See page 106

A MOVABLE FEAST OF CONTEMPORARY ART
Contemporary art tour of Paris
See page 108

SATURDAY, BUT ALSO EVERY EVENING

THERE WAS A GUY TAKING A SHOWER ... !   **9**
Raidd Bar – 23, rue du Temple 75003 Paris – See page 28

LE MULTICOLORE: LA ROULETTE PARISIENNE   **10**
See page 114

THE COLOUR OF MONEY   **11**
Cercle Clichy-Montmartre. 84, rue de Clichy 75009 Paris – See page 56

A PHONE BOX UNLIKE ANY OTHER...   **12**
Sophie Calle's phone box
Pont du Garigliano 75015 Paris – See page 82

"HOUZE" OF HAPPINESS   **13**
La Maizon – 13, rue Collette 75017 Paris – See page 92

NIGHT OF ADORATION AT SACRÉ-CŒUR   **14**
35, rue du Chevalier-de-la-Barre 75018 Paris – See page 94

BREAKING THE ICE AT 5 BELOW ZERO   **15**
Ice Bar de l'hôtel Kube – 1-5, passage Ruelle 75018 Paris – See page 100

MUSÉE DE L'ÉROTISME   **16**
72, boulevard de Clichy 75018 Paris – See page 133

CRASHING CELEBRITY PARTIES WITH THE SYNDICAT DU HYPE
See page 109

ENJOY YOUR FIFTEEN MINUTES OF FAME
Soirée de star – See page 110

REVISIT PARIS IN A 2CV CONVERTIBLE
"Deux-chevaux" rides around Paris with 4 Roues sous 1 Parapluie – See page 116

A ZODIAC BENEATH THE STARS
Zodiac rides on the Seine, and along the Ourcq and Saint-Martin canals – Voir page 118

ON THE TRAIL OF THE "CATAPHILES"
Clandestine walk in the catacombs – See page 124

PLAY GOLF RIGHT ACROSS PARIS
Streetgolf with 19ème Trou – See page 126

INVITE A PSYCHIC INTO YOUR LIVING ROOM
Paranormal demonstrations with Erick Fearson
See page 71

EVENING SWIMMING
Pools – See page 134

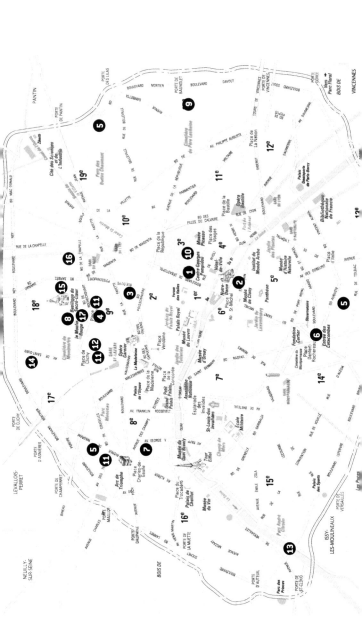

IMAGINE WHAT IT'S LIKE TO BE BLIND ...
DINE IN PITCH BLACKNESS
Dans le Noir

51, rue Quincampoix 75004 Paris
See page 34

❶

TAKE A NAP IN A BOOKSHOP
The bed at Shakespeare & Company, the English-language bookshop

37, rue de la Bûcherie 75005 Paris
See page 38

❷

« ALTHOUGH YOU MAKE MONEY IN THE MÉTRO,
IT'S MORE REWARDING ON STAGE!"
Open stage at the FIEALD

14, rue de Trévise 75009 Paris
See page 54

❸

MUST BE SEEN TO BE BELIEVED
Escualita: transsexual evenings at the Folies Pigalle

Folie's Pigalle – 11, place Pigalle 75009 Paris
See page 58

❹

A CURIOUS BELGIAN FAITH ...
Temple antoiniste

See page 78

❺

JIM'LL FIX IT
Jim Haynes – Sunday Dinners

Métro Alésia ou Saint-Jacques, RER Denfert-Rochereau
See page 80

❻

DELVING INTO THE SECRETS OF THE GREAT ARCHITECT
Loge unie des théosophes

11 bis, rue Kepler 75116 Paris
See page 84

❼

SUNDAY CINEMA AT MARLUSSE ET LAPIN
Screenings every Sunday at 17.00

14, rue Germain Pilon 75018 Paris
See page 67

❽

ALTERNATIVE PUPPETRY AND EXPERIMENTAL MUSIC
Théâtre l'Ogresse

4, rue des Prairies – angle 125, rue de Bagnolet 75020 Paris
See page 106

❾

SUNDAY, BUT ALSO EVERY EVENING

THERE WAS A GUY TAKING A SHOWER … ! ❿
Raidd Bar – 23, rue du Temple 75003 Paris – See page 28

LE MULTICOLORE: LA ROULETTE PARISIENNE ⓫
See page 114

THE COLOUR OF MONEY ⓬
Cercle Clichy-Montmartre. 84, rue de Clichy 75009 Paris – See page 56

A PHONE BOX UNLIKE ANY OTHER… ⓭
Sophie Calle's phone box
Pont du Garigliano 75015 Paris – See page 82

"HOUZE" OF HAPPINESS ⓮
La Maizon – 13, rue Collette 75017 Paris – See page 92

NIGHT OF ADORATION AT SACRÉ-CŒUR ⓯
35, rue du Chevalier-de-la-Barre 75018 Paris – See page 94

BREAKING THE ICE AT 5 BELOW ZERO ⓰
Ice Bar de l'hôtel Kube – 1-5, passage Ruelle 75018 Paris – See page 100

MUSÉE DE L'ÉROTISME ⓱
72, boulevard de Clichy 75018 Paris – See page 133

CRASHING CELEBRITY PARTIES WITH THE SYNDICAT DU HYPE
See page 109

ENJOY YOUR FIFTEEN MINUTES OF FAME
Soirée de star – See page 110

REVISIT PARIS IN A 2CV CONVERTIBLE
"Deux-chevaux" rides around Paris with 4 Roues sous 1 Parapluie – See page 116

A ZODIAC BENEATH THE STARS
Zodiac rides on the Seine, and along the Ourcq and Saint-Martin canals – Voir page 118

ON THE TRAIL OF THE "CATAPHILES"
Clandestine walk in the catacombs – See page 124

PLAY GOLF RIGHT ACROSS PARIS
Streetgolf with 19ème Trou – See page 126

INVITE A PSYCHIC INTO YOUR LIVING ROOM
Paranormal demonstrations with Erick Fearson
See page 71

EVENING SWIMMING
Pools – See page 134

ALPHABETICAL INDEX

Acknowledgements

Our thanks to:

Jean-Sébastien d'Aboville, Altiz, Florence Amiel, Dan Assayag, Association Contraste, Céline Avril, Bruno de Baecque, Émile de Beaumont, Kees and Aude van Beek, Florent Billioud, Antoine Blachez, Philippe Bonfils, Christine Bonneton, Ludovic Bonneton, Jean-Claude Boulliard, Louis-Marie Bourgeois, Jean-Baptiste Bourgeois, Geneviève Brasc-Bautier, Claude Carrau, Dominique Charneau, Julien Chaussé, Muriel Colin-Barrand, Céline Colombani, Philippe Darmayan, Bryce Davesne, Freddy Debize, Stéphane Decaux, Frédéric Duguet, Nadine Eghels, Charles Eon, Agnès and Mikael Eon, Anne Esambert, Marguerite-Marie Formeny, Vincent Formeny, Stéphanie Foucard, Philippe Gloaguen, Amaël Gohier, Azmina Goulamaly, Romaine Guérin, Patrick Haas, Elvire Haberman, Jim Haynes, Amande In, Patrick Ingiliz, Aliette Jalenques, Antoine Jonglez, Aurélie Jonglez, Stéphanie and Guillaume Jonglez, Timothée Jonglez, Stéphanie Kergall, Suzanne de Lacotte, Ghislain de La Hitte, Gilles Lajotte, Benoît de Larouzière, Guillaume du Laurent, Hervé du Laurent, Julien Le Bigot, Jean-Michel Le Cléac'h, Olivier Lefranc, Xavier Lefranc, Odile Le Fur, Marcel and Macaq, Bruno Marguerite, Elena Mashkova, Sophie Mestchersky, Miss Benny, Clément Moulet, Karine Mourot, Francis Ogier and La SAF, Chistophe Omnes, Lucas d'Orgeval, Otto and vodkacola, Sarah Pasquier, Georges Peberel, Marianne and Fabrice Perreau-Saussine, François and Sally Picard, Valérie Picard, Cédric Pilard, Patricia de Pimodan, Laure Plisson, Michel Ravassard, Valérie Renaud, Stéphanie Rivoal, Dominique Roger, Arnaud Rohmer, Ewa Rutkowski, Bertrand Saint Guilhem, Dimitri Salmon, Pierre Santoul, Damien Seyrieix, Catherine Small, Corinne Stampfli, Micheline Terquem, Ambroise Tézenas, Marie-Christine Valla, Delphine Valluet, Martin Vielajus, Henri Villeroy, Raphaëlle and Matthieu Vincent, Karine Zacharias, and all those who opened their doors to us in the course of this titanic task.

Photo credits:

All photos by **Jean-Laurent Cassely**, except:

Jean-Sébastien d'Aboville: p. 124; Ludovic Bourgeois : pp. 22, 26, 27, 44, 158, 168; Julien Chaussé: p. 64; Jacques Garance: pp. 47, 95, 114; Amande In: p. 43; Clément Moulet: pp. 28, 54, 55, 56; Stéphanie Rivoal: pp. 48, 49, 50, 51, 94.

© Centre culturel suédois: pp. 10, 11; © Yoba: p. 12; © Maachi Djelani: pp. 18, 19; © Incognito: p. 42; © C.o.n.s.o.l.e.: pp. 62, 63; © maison-hantée.com : pp. 70, 150; © Christian Richard (Cheval Français): pp. 74,75, 162; © Soirée de star: pp. 110, 111; © Ademas: p. 120; Design graphique © Catherine Pioli: p. 129; Hôtel des Saints-Pères © Antoine Frich: p. 131; © Marché International de Rungis, pp. 142, 143; © 4 roues sous 1 parapluie: p. 172.

Cover: © Christian Richard (Cheval Français).

Cartography: J.-B. Nény – **Editor:** Oriane du Laurent – **Design:** Roland Deloi – **Layout:** Stéphanie Benoit – **Copy-editing/Proof-reading:** Caroline Lawrence – **English translation:** Thomas Clegg – **Distribution:** Michelin

© **JONGLEZ 2008**
ISBN: 978-2-9158-0748-6

Printed in France by Mame - 37000 Tours